WELCOME TO

Paris, the City of Light, is arguably the most beautiful city in the world. If you're not quite convinced, then take a trip down the Seine as the river passes under the splendid Pont des Arts and Pont Alexandre-III, making its triumphal march past such wonders as Notre-Dame, the Tuileries Garden, the Orsay Museum, the Eiffel Tower and the Palais de Chaillot. The capital is surprisingly small within the confines of its ring road: eleven miles from east to west, and less than six miles from north to south – a distance that can be covered on foot in two hours. It is sometimes said that Paris is a village, or at least a series of several villages, each with its own bakery, café, grocery store and square. This is the charm of a city that is both grandiose and personal. The Seine has two banks to explore, the Left and Right Bank, each with its own rhythm and lifestyle: the literary and increasingly fashionable St-Germain; the quintessentially Parisian Montmartre and Pigalle; the mix of working-class and bohemian Canal St-Martin and Oberkampf; and the multi-cultural Belleville. On both sides, however, there is a wealth of bistros, gourmet restaurants, unpretentious cafés, trendy boutiques, adventurous music venues, theaters and colorful street markets. Come and discover all the magic Paris has to offer with this MapGuide!

CONTENTS

Unmissable sights

⭐ Notre-Dame Cathedral

A Gothic masterpiece

THE CATHEDRAL (**A** E2)
→ *6, pl. Jean-Paul-II (4th)*
Tel. 01 42 34 56 10; notredamedeparis.fr
The cathedral is closed for an indefinite period

Notre-Dame stands majestically on the Île de la Cité, between two branches of the Seine. The first impression is one of solemn grandeur: the cathedral is 420 ft long and 108 ft high, and the transept is 157 ft wide. Its construction was initiated in 1163 by the Bishop of Paris, Maurice de Sully, and it continued for more than a century. In keeping with the canons of the emerging Gothic style (largely formulated in the earlier Saint Stephen's Cathedral in Sens and the abbey church in Saint-Denis), the 'stone vessel' features ribbed vaults, flying buttresses, pinnacles and abutments. Situated close to the Louvre Palace, Notre-Dame became the 'parish of French history' and the stage for epochal events, such as the historic marriage of the Catholic Marguerite de Valois and the Protestant Henri de Navarre in 1572, and the coronation of Napoleon I in 1804. A bronze star

embedded in the forecourt marks both the center of Paris and kilometer zero of national roads. The mystique of Notre-Dame attracted record numbers of visitors (almost 13 million per year) – until 15 April, 2019, when a fire destroyed its roof and spire, which brought some of the vault with it as it toppled over. The basic structure and the two towers remained intact, however, and most of the artworks and treasures inside could be saved. The incident shook French society, and promises were immediately made to rebuild the cathedral by 2024. Until then, the interior will be out of bounds, but there is still plenty to see on its exterior.

Main façade

This is divided into three sections, each with monumental portals decorated with bas-reliefs. These are topped by 28 statues of the Kings of Judah, and above them a rose window is framed by two arched windows. The sculptures on the façade were (like the steeple) heavily vandalized during the French Revolution but they were subsequently restored in the 19th century by Eugène Viollet-le-Duc, who took the opportunity to depict himself among both the Kings of Judah (eighth from the left) and the apostles at the foot of the steeple (he can be seen turning toward it). Before the fire, a spire designed by Viollet-le-Duc soared to a height of 305 ft to the rear.

Towers

Both the cathedral's 226-ft towers date back to the 13th century, but the southern one was built several years earlier, and close examination reveals differences between these seemingly identical structures. The south tower, for example, boasts the cathedral's biggest bell, which weighs 13 tons. The first levels of the two towers are linked by the famous Chimera Gallery, adorned with phantasmagorical, often grotesque statues that seem to keep watch over the building. Viollet-le-Duc gave full rein to his inventive spirit here, particularly with the Stryge, a renowned half-woman, half-bird demon looking over Paris with her chin on her hands. (Stand back from the building to see the chimeras fully.) The chimeras are purely decorative but the gargoyles tucked under the roof serve to drain off rain water (these are also visible from below).

✪ Luxembourg Gardens

A tranquil idyll

THE GARDENS (A B3)
→ *2, rue Auguste-Comte (6th)*
Daily sunrise–sunset

This beautiful park, much beloved by generations of Parisians, was commissioned in 1612 by Queen Marie de' Medici, who sought to recreate a small piece of Italy as a refuge from the intrigues of the Louvre Palace. It was designed by Jacques Boyceau, the pioneering theorist of the French-style garden. Its central section is composed of a huge circular flowerbed crowned by terraces and perfectly geometric paths that prolong the lines of the palace. The overall effect is one of order and domination of Nature. In the 19th century, new gardens were added, this time designed in the English style. The park's location close to the Sorbonne and the schools in the Latin Quarter has made it popular with students ever since it was opened to the public in 1778. It is also a wonderful playground for children, with pony and horse rides, puppet shows and remote-controlled miniature boats on the large octagonal pond.

Sculptures
The gardens constitute a veritable open-air museum dotted with 106 sculptures, mainly dating from the 19th century. The pond is framed by a series of white marble *Queens of France and Illustrious Women*. To the west of the palace there is a fountain (1890) designed as a tribute to Eugène Delacroix by Jules Dalou.

Medici Fountain
This majestic Italian style portico (1630), nestling underneath plane trees, overlooks a 164-ft-long pond, which was complemented in the 19th century by a sculpture created by Auguste Ottin depicting the cyclops Polyphemus surprising the nymph Galatea in the arms of a shepherd, Acis.

LUXEMBOURG PALACE
→ *15, rue de Vaugirard (6th)*
Tel. 01 42 34 20 00; senat.fr
Open to visits Mon and Fri; Free admission

After the assassination of Henri IV, Queen Marie de' Medici was quick to abandon the Louvre and commissioned Salomon de Brosse to build a new, 'Florentine' palace on land on the edge of the city previously owned by François de Luxembourg. This elegant Renaissance masterpiece, completed in 1622, was inspired by the Palazzo Pitti in Florence but also borrowed the traditional layout of a French château: an inner courtyard, a main building and two side pavilions. After the Day of the Dupes (1630), in which the young Louis XIII seized power and sent the Queen Mother into exile, the palace became the property of the Orléans family. It served as a prison during the Terror, before being refurbished under the Consulate, which turned it into the Senate in 1799 (a function that it still retains today). The whole complex was further remodeled in the 19th century. The senate chamber and the library decorated by Eugène Delacroix (complete with 57,000 books) are well worth a visit.

LUXEMBOURG MUSEUM
→ *19, rue de Vaugirard (6th)*
Tel. 01 40 13 62 00; museeduluxembourg.fr
Exhibitions: Daily 10.30am–7pm (10pm Fri)
Admission €13

France's first public art museum, set in a wing of the palace's orangery, opened in 1750 and originally displayed paintings from the royal collection. As these were later absorbed by the Louvre, the museum no longer has a permanent collection but instead organizes ambitious temporary exhibitions.

⭐ Centre Georges-Pompidou

Top-ranking cultural institution

THE CENTER (B C3)
→ Pl. Georges-Pompidou (4th)
Tel. 01 44 78 12 33
centrepompidou.fr
National Museum of Modern Art: Wed–Mon 11am–9pm (11pm Thu for temporary exhibitions); Admission €14
Brancusi's studio: Wed–Mon 2–6pm; Free admission

The innovative architecture of Renzo Piano and Richard Rogers establishes the guiding principles of fantasy, audacity and creativity for this major cultural hub, which houses a skeleton of brightly colored tubes (blue for air-conditioning, green for fluids, red for circulation of people, yellow for electricity) and a 'caterpillar' escalator shrouded in glass. It met with immediate success after its opening in 1977. Every day more than 25,000 people visit the various parts of the center, which establish dialogues between visual art, dance, theater, music, cinema and literature. The modern art collection is the largest in Europe and it is complemented by prestigious temporary exhibitions, a public library, a musical creation area and auditoria for cinema and performances.

The former French president, after whom the center is named, wanted it to be a lively, democratic and unstuffy space, and accordingly there is always something going on here: workshops for children, guided tours of the collections and the building, screenings, lectures, debates, festivals and concerts.

National Museum of Modern Art
The museum's permanent collection numbers more than 100,000 items, with over 1,100 on display, offering a wide-ranging overview of art from the 20th and 21st centuries. On the 4th floor, the contemporary art collection (featuring work produced after 1960) combines large-scale installations, photographs, sculptures and paintings in a thematic journey that is regularly renewed. Certain rooms focus on a specific movement (kinetic art, Fluxus, outsider art) while others hone in on a particular artist or theme (feminism, dance). On the 5th floor, masterpieces from the modern art collection provide a chronological illustration of the major artistic movements from 1905 to 1960. So, the pure colors of the Fauves (André Derain, *Notation on a setting sun*; Henri Matisse, *The Gypsy*) are juxtaposed with the geometrical experiments of the Cubists (Pablo Picasso, *The Guitarist*; Georges Braque, *The Viaduct in L'Estaque*; Fernand Léger, *The Wedding*) and the visionary brain-scrambling of the Surrealists (Salvador Dalí, *Invisible Sleeping Woman, Horse, Lion*; Max Ernst, *Ubu Imperator*; Joan Miró, *The Siesta*), as well as numerous examples of abstraction (Kandinsky, Mondrian), Pop Art (Warhol), Arte Povera and much more besides. The 6th floor is given over to blockbuster shows, while also providing stunning views of the city.

Brancusi's studio
The Romanian artist Constantin Brancusi (1876–1957) lived and worked in Paris from 1904 until his death, and he bequeathed his entire studio (with completed works, sketches, furniture, tools etc.) to the French state in 1956. The present reconstruction, built by Renzo Piano, provides a captivating view into the minimalist universe of this key figure of early 20th-century sculpture. The studio contains 137 of his sculptures (including the famous gilded bronze *Danaïde*, 1913), along with plinths, sketches and numerous photographic plates and prints.

✪ Louvre Museum

World-famous repository of artworks, from ancient times to the 19th century

THE MUSEUM (C E3)
→ Cour Napoléon (1st)
Tel. 01 40 20 50 50; louvre.fr
Wed-Mon 9am–6pm (9.45pm Wed, Fri and first Sat of each month); Admission €15 (free entry first Sat of each month after 6pm)

For almost eight centuries the Louvre served as a royal palace and seat of political power but now it is a museum that attracts millions of visitors every year to its extraordinary art collections. It would take a full week to cover the entire selection, which ranges from universal masterpieces to everyday objects from the past. The journey round the museum also constitutes a trip through the Louvre itself, from its construction in 1190 as a defensive fortress to its successive enlargements over the centuries, its abandonment by Louis XIV in favor of Versailles and its conversion into a museum in 1793. From 1985–89, the Napoleon Courtyard saw the construction of a spectacular glass pyramid designed by Ieoh Ming Pei, which thrust the Louvre into the contemporary era. The museum's 35,000 artworks are spread over eight departments and three connected wings (Sully to the east, Richelieu to the north, Denon to the south).

The Middle Ages
The basement of the Sully wing displays the remnants of the medieval Louvre. The unearthing of the foundations of the original ramparts has shed considerable light on the various stages of the building's construction.

Antiquities
The jaw-dropping collection of Ancient Egyptian artifacts is particularly exemplified by the famous limestone statue of the *Seated Scribe* (room 22). The Greek, Roman and Etruscan antiquities are no less impressive, thanks to works like the *Milet Torso* (room 3), the legendary *Venus de Milo* (room 16) and the *Winged Victory of Samothrace*. There are also antiquities from further east, including Assyrian reliefs from the Khorsabad Court and the superb *Frieze of Archers* from the palace of the Persian king Darius the Great.

Sculptures
The Richelieu wing traces the story of French sculpture, from Roman times to monumental works from the 19th century (some on display in the glass-covered Marly and Puget courtyards). The Denon wing focuses on Italian sculpture: Michelangelo (*Dying Slave*, room 4), Bernini, Canova.

Paintings
The museum contains over 1,000 paintings, with 77 rooms devoted to French painting alone. All the expected heavyweights are represented: Poussin, Watteau, Chardin, Fragonard, Delacroix, Géricault (*The Raft of the Medusa*). Part of the Italian section features the museum's biggest crowd puller, the *Mona Lisa*. The Richelieu wing gathers together, under the heading of the Northern Schools, works by Rubens, Rembrandt and Vermeer.

Fine art objects
Highlights include the Crown Jewels, in the Apollo gallery, and the 'Regent', a famous 140-carat diamond; and Napoleon III's apartments, a unique example of Second Empire interior decoration.

Graphic art
Over 130,000 drawings, pastels and prints, by artists including Leonardo da Vinci, Michelangelo and Dürer.

Islamic art
The most recently created department is set in the restored Visconti courtyard.

✪ Musée d'Orsay

A temple to Impressionism (and beyond)

THE MUSEUM (C C4)

→ 1, rue de la Légion-d'Honneur (7th)
Tel. 01 40 49 48 14; musee-orsay.fr
Tue-Sun 9.30am–6pm (9.45pm Thu)
Admission €12

The creation of this museum in the 1980s breathed new life into the old Orsay train station, a stone and metal masterpiece created by Victor Laloux for the 1900 Universal Exhibition. The great hall's stunning glass roof reflects the period's engineering prowess, while the groundbreaking artistic innovations that sent out shock waves from 1848 to 1914 are in evidence below it in the form of sculpture, painting, photographs, architecture and decorative arts. Official academic art was swept away by the Impressionists (who are represented here by a collection unequalled anywhere in the world). Other rooms focus on the decorative arts, including superb examples of Art Nouveau, while newer spaces resulting from the museum's facelift in 2011 are given over to prestigious temporary exhibitions.

Sculpture

Both the central aisle dividing the ground floor and its mid-level side terraces trace the various branches of sculpture that emerged in the 19th century: neoclassicism inspired by ancient art (Eugène Guillaume), impetuous and expressive Romanticism (David d'Angers) and eclecticism (see the *Dance* and *Ugolin* by Jean-Baptiste Carpeaux). These were succeeded by realism, Impressionism (represented by Edgar Degas' *Little Dance of Fourteen Years*) and the emergence of modern sculpture through Auguste Rodin (*Balzac*) and Camille Claudel (*Age of Maturity*), which in turn provoked a return to classicism and formal simplification in Aristide Maillol (*The Mediterranean*), François Pompon (*White Bear*) and Antoine Bourdelle (*Hercules the Archer*).

Painting

In the ground-floor rooms, Ingres and Delacroix fly the flag for academicism, whose tenets were called into question in 1863 by the Salon des Refusés: from then on, genres once considered minor (landscape, still life) became synonymous with modernity, especially in the hands of realists like Millet (*The Gleaners*) and Courbet (whose *Origin of the World* shocked his contemporaries) or Symbolists like Puvis de Chavanne, whose paintings emanate a haunting strangeness.

On the 5th floor, the museum's centerpiece, the Impressionists' gallery, displays an extraordinary collection by Cézanne, Renoir (*Dance at the Moulin de la Galette*), Monet (*Rouen Cathedral* series) and Degas, as well as Sisley and Pisarro, who further invigorated painting through their innovative use of color and light. The 2nd floor shows Impressionism's fruitful afterlife: its fragmentary approach gave rise to the Divisionism of Seurat (*The Circus*) and inspired some of Van Gogh's greatest masterpieces (*Church in Auvers-sur-Oise*).

Decorative arts

Furniture dominates here, but there is also pottery and objects made of glass and metal (crockery, vases, lamps, mirrors). Highlights are the various European branches of Art Nouveau: English Arts and Crafts, the Glasgow School, the Viennese Jugendstil, etc. A reconstruction of a dining room designed by Alexandre Charpentier is particularly sumptuous, as are Gallé's *Dragonfly Vitrine* and the furniture used by the Duchess of Parma for her *toilette*.

✪ Sacré-Cœur

An emblematic monument on the peak of Montmartre

THE BASILICA (D C3)

➔ *35, rue du Chevalier-de-la-Barre (18th)*
Tel. 01 53 41 89 00; sacre-coeur-montmartre.com
Daily 6am–10.30pm; free admission
Dome (entrance on left side of the basilica):
Oct-April: Daily 9am–5pm; May-Sep: Daily 8.30am–8pm
Admission €6

The unmistakable outline of the Sacré-Coeur Basilica looms over Paris from the summit of Montmartre. It has a unique, otherworldly quality, derived from the combination of a Greek-cross layout with an uninhibited approach to Romano-Byzantine architecture that juxtaposes spires and domes, all exuding a pristine whiteness (due to the calcite secreted by the stone when it comes into contact with rainwater). The interior is equally mesmerizing, although a visit requires a climb up Montmartre's famously vertigo-inducing (albeit extremely charming) streets and some steep flights of steps.

The will of the nation

In 1873 France was reeling after a series of national disasters: its defeat by Prussia and the loss of Alsace-Lorraine in 1871 and, the following year, the uprising of the Paris Commune, which wreaked havoc on the city. The construction of a basilica dedicated to the Sacred Heart of Christ was considered an expiatory gesture in the public good and it was approved by the National Assembly. The site chosen for the building was highly symbolic: Montmartre had already been sanctified by the martyrdom of Saint Denis in the 3rd century and, moreover, it had been the starting point for the rebellion of the Commune. The basilica's spiritual vocation remains strong today and it has become a significant pilgrimage site.

An onerous construction process

The construction work, which was entirely financed by voluntary donations, began in 1876 under the supervision of the architect Paul Abadie, who was immediately confronted with technical challenges. The hill's subsoil was riddled with galleries left from years of mining for 'montmartrite' (gypsum). Abadie was obliged to reinforce the foundations with 83 pillars descending to a depth of 125 ft: hence the joke that the basilica is holding up the hill, rather than the other way round! After 30 years and a succession of six architects, the Sacré-Coeur was completed on the eve of World War One, but it would have to wait until 1919 for its consecration.

Interior

Entering through the porch (topped with equestrian statues of Joan of Arc and Saint Louis), visitors are understandably struck by the largest mosaic in France (over 5,000 sq. ft), set above the choir. Designed by Luc-Olivier Merson, it depicts the Holy Trinity, including Christ with a glowing heart. The visual impact is further enhanced by the organ, with its 5,384 pipes, and the imposing crypt, which contains tombs and sacred relics. A small side room houses an audiovisual display documenting the building's construction.

Dome and bell tower

The Sacré-Coeur dome provides one of the city's highest vantage points, rivalled only by the Eiffel and Montparnasse towers, but the panoramic views can only be enjoyed after a steep climb of 300 steps. Alongside, the 276-ft bell tower (known as the 'minaret') was the work of the building's penultimate architect, Lucien Magne. It houses the *Savoyarde* (1895), which weighs 19 tons, making it one of the heaviest bells in the world: thirty horses were required to haul it up the hill!

✪ Champs-Élysées

Boulevard linking the Place de la Concorde and the Arc de Triomphe

THE AVENUE (E D3-F4)

The 'most beautiful avenue in the world' stretches for over a mile between the Louvre and La Défense, taking in several major historical institutions. Nowadays, it is more often associated with luxury hotels and stores, and with theaters and cabarets, but it still bears witness to the pioneering modernity and elegance of the 1920s. The boulevard remains vibrant long after the stores close thanks to its cinemas, nightclubs and concert halls. It also provides a stage for official parades, demonstrations and public celebrations. Increased car ownership in the last century led to overly dense parking on the Champs-Élysées but a major refurbishment in 1994 tackled the problem, and the avenue is now kept free of cars on the first Sunday of every month.

Points of interest

At the southern end of the Champs-Élysées, the hectic Place de la Concorde (**E** A4) is dominated by the Luxor Obelisk and framed by vistas of the Louvre, on the one side, and the Arc de Triomphe on the other. Before reaching a traffic circle, the avenue is lined with gardens, interrupted by the Petit Palais and then the Grand Palais (**E** E4). After that, stores, restaurants and cafés take over, including the legendary Fouquet's at no. 99: its superb dining room, now officially declared a heritage site, was a favorite meeting place of directors from the French New Wave in the 1960s. Across the road, at no. 101, the Louis Vuitton store is graced by contemporary art and an arresting pitch-black elevator designed by the Danish artist Olafur Eliasson. At no. 133, the renowned Drugstore Publicis has been stylishly refitted by Michele Saee in glass and steel. Finally, the Lido, where Édith Piaf, Marlene Dietrich and Joséphine Baker once trod the boards, has been at no. 116 bis since 1977. It had previously been located at no. 78, under arcades whose pink marble columns and Venetian-style Lalique lamps can still be seen.

ARC DE TRIOMPHE (E C3)

→ *Pl. Charles-de-Gaulle (entrance via a pedestrian tunnel from the avenue des Champs-Élysées and from the avenue de la Grande-Armée (8th)*
paris-arc-de-triomphe.fr
Oct-March: Daily 10am–10.30pm
April-Sep: Daily 10am–11pm
Free admission (charge for top section and roof €12)

Napoleon spared no expense when commissioning a monument in honor of his 'Great Army' in 1806: he wanted a triumphal arch that would dominate Paris, proclaim his taste for all things Roman and guarantee his place in history. When it was finally opened in 1836, during the reign of Louis-Philippe, the arch had been reconceived and was intended to celebrate France's military exploits during the Revolution and the First Empire. As a memorial for soldiers killed in combat, the arch is an obligatory port-of-call in any official event extolling national achievements. A flame is rekindled every night to keep watch over the tomb of the Unknown Soldier.

Bas-reliefs

These depict scenes from the revolutionary and Napoleonic wars. Four large-scale allegories decorate the lower section of the arch. François Rude's *Marseillaise* is particularly expressive.

Attic

Just below the terrace (with its stunning view of the Champs-Élysées from above), a multimedia installation explains the significance of the various bas-reliefs and statues that adorn the arch.

⭐ Eiffel Tower

The instantly recognizable symbol of Paris

THE TOWER (F D1)

→ *Champ-de-Mars Av. Gustave-Eiffel (7th)*
Tel. 01 44 11 23 23
toureiffel.paris
Mid June–early Sep: Daily 9am–12.45am
Early Sep–mid June: Daily 9.30am–11.45pm
(Online reservation advised, 2-3 months in advance)
Elevator charges €16 (2nd floor), €25 (3rd floor);
staircase charge €10 (2nd floor)

The Eiffel Tower has acquired an unrivalled iconic status, so, of all the city's monuments with admission charges, it is the one that receives the most visitors: over 6 million per year. It is easy to forget, therefore, that it once had critics who vehemently called for its destruction even before it had been finished in time for the 1899 Universal Exhibition. Eiffel's project had been selected from a total of 107 submissions, but many commentators considered it little more than glorified scaffolding: it was deemed 'monstrous and useless', an eyesore that heaped 'dishonor' on Paris. A petition launched to truncate its construction was signed by luminaries such as Maupasssant, Verlaine and Zola. Undaunted, Gustave Eiffel and his team of 50 engineers and 132 workers (endowed with acrobatic skills) labored on for 26 months to assemble the 18,000 pieces required to bring his design to fruition. Its industrial esthetic symbolized the grandeur and power of France in that era of technical progress and international rivalries: the Eiffel Tower conserved its title of the world's highest building right up to the completion of the Empire State Building...in 1931. The tower was originally destined to stay up for 20 years only but it escaped demolition thanks to its use as a telegraphic relay mast that had played a key role in World War One. In 1921 it became a radio station, before being turned into a television antenna in 1950 (a function that it continues to honour today).

Ground level

Don't be put off by the long lines at the ticket office – instead, take the opportunity to survey the tower's structure from below – and admire, near the north pillar, a gilded bust of Eiffel himself, sculpted in 1929 by Antoine Bourdelle.

First and second floors

The 1st and 2nd floors, respectively 187 and 377 ft high, can be reached by the elevators in the north and west pillars or by the 704 steps in the south pillar. It is easy to experience vertigo, even on the 1st floor, which is fitted with a transparent floor that gives the impression of walking over a void. The exterior at this level is engraved with the names of prominent scientific figures from the 18th and 19th centuries, such as André-Marie Ampère (whose surname now denotes a unit of electrical current). There is also a restaurant, buffet and souvenir store.

On the 2nd floor, animated display cases trace the various phases of the tower's construction, while the restaurant, Le Jules Verne, is a more up-market affair, run by the star chef Alain Ducasse.

Third floor

Only accessible by elevator, the third and last floor (905 ft high) offers exceptional views (extending for over 35 miles on a fine day), a small champagne bar and a reconstruction of Gustave Eiffel's office.

⭐ Parc de la Villette

Music, science, themed gardens and a whole host of activities

THE PARK (J C2-D2)
→ avillette.com; Daily, 24hrs

The former slaughterhouses and meat market of La Villette (set on either side of the Ourcq Canal) now provide the stage for an innovative park. It was part of an ambitious scheme drawn up by Bernard Tschumi in 1987 to develop this part of East Paris, with culture, architecture and Nature as its watchwords. The project was distinguished by its meticulous attention to detail and its break with tradition with regard to colors, forms and textures. The undulating canopy of the Galerie de la Villette connects the City of Science and Industry (to the north) with that of Music (to the south), while also leading to the metal covered market that is now used for cultural events. Paths paved in blue wind their way through gardens designed around themes (bamboo, dragons, mirrors, childhood fears), some of which double as playgrounds. The park is divided into sections by means of 26 red follies, each with its own distinctive architecture (with restaurants, information points and performance spaces).

In summer, a giant screen is set up on the Triangle Field for an open-air film festival.

CITÉ DE LA MUSIQUE – PHILHARMONIE DE PARIS (J D2)
→ 221, av. Jean-Jaurès (19th)
Tel. 01 44 84 44 84; philharmoniedeparis.fr
Tue-Sun noon (10am Sat-Sun)–6pm
Museum admission €8

To the southeast of the park, this huge complex devoted to music was drawn up in 1995 by Christian de Portzamparc. Its program is highly eclectic and incorporates many educational activities: concerts (some by the resident Orchestra of Paris), workshops, lectures and a multimedia library. Its museum traces a musical journey from the Renaissance to the present day through more than 1,000 instruments, models and artworks. In 2015 the City of Music was complemented by the eye-catching Philarmonie, designed by Jean Nouvel with shimmering swathes of aluminum in various shades of gray. The interior is equally impressive, with spaces for temporary exhibitions and a swirling 2,400-seater concert hall. On top, the terrace (open to all) is 122 ft above ground level and affords magnificent views of the city. The approach here is similarly varied and educational: family concerts, workshops and performances specifically aimed at young people.

CITÉ DES SCIENCES ET DE L'INDUSTRIE (J C2)
→ 30, av. Corentin-Cariou (19th)
Tel. 01 40 05 70 00; cite-sciences.fr
Tue-Sun 10am–6pm (7pm Sun); Admission €12

The metal framework and glass walls of this 'city' were dreamed up in 1986 by Adrien Fainsilber, using a former slaughterhouse building as his starting point. The driving force behind this vast complex, set on top of an expanse of water, is the dissemination of scientific knowledge. Various islands focusing on a particular theme (the brain, sound, energy, etc.) are connected to each other by walkways and staircases. A playful and interactive approach serves to make even the most complex topics more accessible. There is also a planetarium, a 3-D cinema and the famous Géode (re-opening in 2020), with a steel sphere 120 ft in diameter encasing one of the largest hemispherical screens in the world.

✪ Bois de Boulogne

The 'green lung' of West Paris, covering an expanse of over three square miles

LE BOIS (OFF MAP E AND F)
→ *Subway: Porte-Maillot, Les Sablons, Porte-Dauphine*
The Bois de Boulogne, the remains of the medieval Rouvray Forest, was once reserved as a royal hunting ground but Louis XIV made it accessible to broader aristocratic circles, which led to the construction of various châteaux, notably those of Neuilly, Bagatelle and the Folie Saint-James. In the late 19th century it began to attract a wider public, thanks to its botanical garden and amusement park, as well as the Longchamps and Auteuil racetracks. These days, its expanse of woodland, lakes, sports facilities and gardens crisscrossed by footpaths and bicycle trails attract Parisians from all walks of life.

AUTEUIL GLASSHOUSES
→ *3, av. de la Porte-d'Auteuil (16th)*
Mon-Fri 8am–sunset, Sat-Sun 9am–sunset
Free admission
Spread around a French-style garden created by Jean-Camille Formigé in 1898, 6,000 plant species grow inside turquoise-tinted glasshouses. The most impressive of these is topped with a central dome and contains palm trees. The glasshouses form part of the Jardin Botanique de Paris.

BAGATELLE PARK
→ *On the road from Sèvres to Neuilly (16th)*
Tel. 01 53 64 53 80
Daily 9.30am–8pm (6.30pm Oct-March, 5pm Nov-Feb)
Admission €2.50 (from May to Oct only)
This other branch of the Jardin Botanique de Paris is particularly renowned for its spectacular rose garden, which boasts almost 10,000 bushes, which come into full bloom in June. The park plays host to an international rose-growing competition, as well as a series of cultural events. There is also an orangery and a Chinese pagoda, not to mention the Château de Bagatelle itself, an elegant neo-Palladian pleasure pavilion. A series of bridges and waterways only add to the park's bucolic charm.

JARDIN D'ACCLIMATATION (E A2)
→ *Tel. 01 40 67 90 85; jardinacclimatation.fr*
Daily 11am (10am Sat-Sun and school vacations)–7pm (6pm Oct-March); Admission €5
Generations of children have taken a boat ride on the Enchanted River, the star attraction of this amusement park opened by Napoleon III in 1860. Its 47 acres gather together old-fashioned merry-go-rounds and real pony rides, an educational farm and puppet shows, plus 17 new attractions that were unveiled in 2018 following renovation.

LOUIS-VUITTON FOUNDATION (E A3)
→ *8, avenue du Mahatma Gandhi (16th)*
Tel. 01 40 69 96 00; fondationlouisvuitton.fr
Mon, Wed-Fri noon–7pm (11pm Fri for night-time events); Sat-Sun 11am–8pm; Admission €16
The Louis Vuitton Foundation opened in 2014 to showcase the outstanding collection of contemporary art amassed by Bernard Arnault, the chairman of the LVMH multinational conglomerate. It comprises works created after 1960, divided into four areas: contemplative, Expressionist, Pop and music/sound. The building itself resembles a boat with glass and metal sails, created by the architect Frank Gehry, who drew inspiration from the 19th-century glasshouses that are so closely associated with the Bois de Boulogne. The foundation also puts on temporary exhibitions, complemented by debates, lectures and concerts.

Paris in 3 days

Capture the essence of the city on a long weekend!

FRIDAY

8.30am Soak up the atmosphere of the Latin Quarter in La Petite Viennoise (**A** C3), very popular with students at breakfast time.

9.30am Stroll amongst the majestic chestnut trees in the Luxembourg Gardens (**A** B3) before visiting the Pantheon (**A** D4); and wander the remaining alleyways of medieval Paris that lead down to the Seine.

10.30am Visit Notre-Dame (**A** E2), the Gothic masterpiece whose facade and superb portals warrant a close look.

11am See the city from a different angle by boarding a Batobus at the Hôtel de Ville stop. Cruise down the Seine, past the Musée d'Orsay (**C** C4) and under emblematic bridges like the Pont-Neuf (**A** C1) and Pont Alexandre-III (**F** F1), with its four socles topped with gilded bronze statues of Fames.

Noon The Eiffel Tower (**F** D1) can be seen from the Trocadéro for its majesty, from below for its elegance and from inside for its unique views of Paris.

1pm Lunch in the Café Constant (**F** E1) or the Café de Mars (**F** E2), two good bistros close to the Eiffel Tower.

2.30pm Cross the Seine via the Pont de l'Alma (**F** E1) and shop for high fashion on Avenue Montaigne (**E** D4).

3pm Head for the Champs-Élysées (**E** E4) for more mainstream shopping – and for an optimum view of the Arc de Triomphe (**E** C3).

3.30pm Take a break in the Tuileries Gardens (**C** C3): sit by the edge of a pond on one of the famous green chairs produced by Fermob.

4.15pm Take tea in the elegant Café Marly (**C** E3), which offers fine views of the imposing pyramid in the Louvre.

5pm Take in the priceless collections at the Louvre (**C** E3). If Impressionism and the 19th century appeal more, then head across the Seine to the Musée d'Orsay (**C** C4).

7pm Start off the evening with a drink in Saint-Germain-des-Prés, either in the Deux Magots café (**A** B2), or on the delightful terrace of the Café de la Mairie (**A** B3), in the shadow of the Saint-Suplice Church.

8.30pm Try dinner (reserve ahead) at Les Pipos (**A** D3) or the more expensive, and equally renowned, Comptoir du Relais Saint-Germain (**A** C2).

10pm Catch a concert (jazz, swing, soul) in the reputed Caveau de la Huchette (**A** D2). Or you may prefer to see a film in one of the arthouse movie theaters in the Latin Quarter.

Midnight You can carry on partying in the bars in the City of Fashion and Design (**H** C3) or onboard the barges docked by the quays near the National Library (**H** C3).

SATURDAY

9am Breakfast in the Loir dans la Théière (**B** E3). The name translates as 'dormouse in the teapot', which gives some idea of the whimsical nature of the place.

10am Explore the Marais, where the traditional mansion houses have now been joined by fashionable art galleries. See *Walks* pages (**K**).

11.30am Revel in the pioneering architecture of the Centre Georges-Pompidou (**B** C3) and its equally extraordinary modern art collection.

1pm Snacks from all over the world (Sicily, Morocco, the Caribbean) are on offer for lunch in the charming Enfants-Rouges Market (**B** E2).

1.45pm Walk through the gardens and arcades of the Hôtel de Soubise (**B** D3) on the way to the Place des Vosges (**B** E4).

2.30pm The Place de la Bastille (**I** B2) carries the weight of history, even if the former fortress has been replaced by the July Column. The numerous small passageways in the Faubourg Saint-Antoine are equally evocative (**I** C3).

3.30pm Take a break in a typical neighborhood meeting place: the Pure Café (**I** C2).

4pm Check out the cutting-edge fashion of brands like Isabel Marant, Sessùn and Soeur in stores on the Rue de la Charonne and the Rue Keller (**I** C2).

5pm A change of pace on the shady paths of the Père-Lachaise cemetery (**I** D2), which is the last resting place of many prominent figures.

7pm The rooftop bar on the 7th floor of Le Perchoir (**I** C1) is a popular rendezvous for an evening drink, with the city coming alight in the background.

8.30pm For dinner: international vegetarian food at Soya (**I** B1), traditional Parisian fare at the Vieux Belleville (**J** C5) or trendy innovation in Le Chateaubriand (**I** B1).

10pm Round off the night with a concert in Le Bellevilloise (**J** D5) or go dancing in the Rosa Bonheur (**J** C4).

SUNDAY

10am Angelina (**C** D2) is said to serve the best hot chocolate in Paris...

11am After taking in the window displays of the top-level jewelry stores on the Place Vendôme and the Rue de la Paix (**D** C2), stroll through the gardens and the arcades of the Palais Royal (**C** E2).

12.30pm Wander around the passageways near the Bibliothèque Nationale (National Library), stopping off at the Japanese restaurant Higuma (**C** E2) on the Rue Sainte-Anne for exceptional ramen. If a ham sandwich is more inviting, head for Le Petit Vendôme (**C** D2).

1.30pm Pass the Opéra Garnier (**C** D1) to reach the Boulevard Haussman, where the department stores open on Sundays. The Galeries Lafayette (**D** A6) is worth seeing for its impressive dome alone.

3pm Mingle with the collectors on the picturesque covered passageways (**D** C6) running off the Grands Boulevards (**D**): philately on the Passage des Panoramas, vintage toys on Passage Jouffroy.

4.30pm Head to Montmartre via the streets in Nouvelle Athènes (**D** B5). En route: Notre-Dame-de-Lorette, the pretty Place Saint-Georges and the Museum of the Romantics (**D** B4), which is free and has a lovely tea shop with a glass roof and terrace sheltered by trees.

5.30pm Tackle the daunting climb up to the forecourt of the Sacré-Coeur (**D** C3), or try the less grueling funicular train. The most intrepid souls can take a further climb up to the dome, and be rewarded with breathtaking views.

6.30pm Take a stroll around the delightful back streets of Montmartre (**D**).

7.30pm The food is unfussy (but tasty) in the Grand 8 (**D** C3) and the views of Montparnasse are great.

9.30pm Head back to Pigalle to sample its nightlife in Dirty Dick (**D** B4), a tiki bar with exotic cocktails. Or catch a show in one of the many local theaters.

AN EXTRA DAY?

An opportunity to stray from the beaten path...
Montparnasse (G)
Following in the steps of Cocteau and Hemingway, take a drink on the terrace of La Coupole (**G** B3) before going to see a play nearby.
Butte-aux-Cailles (H A5)
One of the last remaining Parisian 'villages' to preserve its character: old workers' houses, cobblestones and small family restaurants.
Canal Saint-Martin (J)
This enchanting leafy canal has the usual docks and walkways, as well as stores and cafés that spill on to the quays. See *Walks* (**K**).
Parc de la Villette (J C2)

Themed gardens, the City of Science, and concerts and films in the Philharmonie (**J** D2); outdoor movies in summer.
Saint-Ouen flea markets (off map **D**)
→ *Subway: Porte de Clignancourt; Sat-Sun 9am (10am Sun)–6pm; Mon 11am–5pm*
Search for that once-in-a-lifetime bargain in the maze of stalls of this famous flea market. See *Day Trips* (**L**).
Bois de Vincennes (off map **I**)
→ *Subway: Château de Vincennes*
An escape from the urban scene: woods, a lake, footpaths, a château and the Floral Park. See *Day Trips* (**L**).

LES DEUX MAGOTS

Do as the locals do

Take your place at the zinc counter of a café

Cafés are the center of Parisian social life and, for many, a home away from home. Small neighborhood cafés are perfect for people-watching and for getting a feel of the soul of the city. You'll be spoilt for choice as they are extremely common – there is one café in Paris for every 200 inhabitants. Once spring arrives, it's the start of the season of *en terrasse* lounging and socializing.

→ *Café de la Mairie* (**A** B3), *Pure Café* (**I** C2)

Indulge in an ice cream at Berthillon (**A** F3)

A welcome treat at all times of day, the cornets sold by the city's most famous ice-cream parlor never fail to delight, and they taste even better sitting on the quays of the Île St-Louis. Sorbet and ice cream come in some 75 imaginative flavors: marron glacé, fig, bitter chocolate, Earl Grey tea, gingerbread, pistachio, lemon and coriander, wild strawberry...

→ *In summer, go in the morning to avoid the long queues*

Get around on a Vélib' bicycle

This self-service bicycle rental service has been a huge success since it began operating in 2007. You can experience the city from a new perspective, enjoying its side streets, deserted back alleys and special bike lanes on some of the quays. Some electric models are also now available.

→ *Certain bike stations are always full, especially at night, while others are always empty. See the* **Practicalities** *pages and velib-metropole.fr*

Take the métro

Parisians may complain about the rush hour but they are proud of their subway system, not only for its efficiency but also for its various historic stations and the striking Art Nouveau architecture that has been a feature of the capital's métro since the beginning of the 20th century – museums in their own right. Also, the lines that venture high above ground reveal striking views of the city.

→ *See stations Louvre-Rivoli (copies of paintings from the Louvre), Arts-et-Métiers (designed by François Schuiten), Varenne (dedicated to Rodin); and the aerial lines 2 and 6*

Take a trip on a bâteau-mouche

This is most enjoyable at night, when the crowds have evaporated and the city can be seen from a different perspective, with lights glowing under the bridges and projections from the boat onto the shoreline

TRENDS

The Seine revival

The long-neglected banks of the Seine have come back to life! There are kiosks, barges fitted out for leisure activities, games of *pétanque* (bowls) and concerts. See *Walks* pages (**K**).

Brownfield sites

Abandoned urban wastelands and empty industrial premises have been taken over by cooperatives and become testing grounds for social change, along with the refurbished stations on the Petite Ceinture (a disused railroad track circling the city).

Ground Control (**I** C3)

Rooftops

Haussmann's blueprint for Paris did not envisage a use for rooftops, but more recent buildings have made provision for meeting points above the hubbub of the city. Le Perchoir (**I** C1)

'Neo tapas'

Selections of small portions made for convivial shared eating. Les Petits Plats (**G** B5)

Patisserie frenzy

Choux buns, macaroons, madaleines, brioche, cheesecake...the art of fine pastry-making has reached dizzy heights of sophistication. L'Éclair de génie (**B** E4)

PARTY UNTIL DAWN

PICNIC AT ÎLE ST-LOUIS

that make the buildings come alive.

→ *Look out for the gargoyles on the Pont-Neuf (**A** C1) and the statue (1856) of a Zouave (infantryman) from the Crimean War on the Pont de l'Alma (**F** E1). See also the Practicalities pages*

Lounge at Paris-Plage

Parasols, white sand, deckchairs, *pétanque*, refreshment kiosks, concerts and activities of all kinds – in July and August, the banks of the Seine on the Berge Pompidou (4th) and Bassin de la Villette (19th) turn into a fully fledged beach resort.

→ *Avoid the weekend crowds if possible; try the evenings for a festive feel*

Have a picnic

The arrival of spring is the cue for many Parisians to make their way to a park or riverbank for a picnic – cooked meats, cheese, baguettes and a good bottle of wine in hand.

→ *A perfect spot is Île Saint-Louis (**A** E2)*

Browse the second-hand bookstalls

A two-mile stretch on both sides of the river, running from the Pont Royal to the Pont de Sully, is lined with second-hand bookstalls, 4 ft high and 26 ft wide. They are a treasure trove of old and rare books, magazines, prints, postcards, stamps and comics, embodying a tradition that has

delighted enthusiasts and passersby for four centuries.

→ *Daily approx. 11.30am–sunset; many stalls are closed on rainy days*

Dine at a brasserie

Discover a world seemingly lost in time, from the old retainer opening oyster shells near the door to the team of waiters in their black pants and vests, white shirts and aprons. Relish the traditional classics of French cuisine – bouillabaisse, steak tartare, Alsatian sauerkraut – amid a fabulous decor of Art Deco brass, leather banquettes and mirrors.

→ *La Coupole (**G** B3),*

*La Closerie des Lilas (**G** C3)*

Party until dawn

Paris has a thriving night life, with options to suit all music tastes (indie, techno, hip hop, Latin, disco), from parties on barges in the 13th (**H**) to laid-back bars on the Canal St-Martin (**J**), from the terraces of Oberkampf (**I**) to the student dives of the Latin Quarter (**A**), from the temples of house music on the Grands Boulevards (**D**) to the expensive, ultra-cool clubs of the 8th arrondissement (**E**).

→ *Taxis are few and far between after the subway closes (2am) on Fri and Sat nights*

AT THE BAR

SECOND-HAND BOOKSTALLS

... AND EVEN ON SUNDAYS

Listings
→ *quefaire.paris.fr/weekend*

Markets
→ *Generally 7am–2pm; paris.fr/marches;* see Practicalities pages Food and flea markets.

Brunch
→ *Be sure to book; €20–30* Try Mama Shelter (**I** E2), the BAL Café Otto (**E** F2) or the Jacquemart-André Café (**E** E3).

The 104 (**J** B2)
→ *104.fr/en*
This lively municipal arts center offers exhibitions, break dancing... and a pizza truck.

Shopping
→ *Generally 11am–7pm*

Neighborhoods with Sunday shopping: Marais (**B**), Abbesses (**D** B4), Champs-Élysées (**E** D3), canal Saint-Martin (**J** A4).

'Paris respire'
Areas closed to traffic on Sundays are Montmartre (**D**) and Marais (**B**); and on the first Sun of the month: the Champs-Élysées and the 1st, 2nd, 3rd and 4th arr.

Matinée shows
→ *offi.fr*
In the morning or afternoon: with kids at the Théâtre Chatelet (**B** B3), or at the Opéra Garnier (**C** D1) and the Opéra Bastille (**I** B3).

Paris on a budget

Tips for enjoying the city for less!

FREE

National museums

Certain museums are free all year for teachers and under 26-year-olds, and for everybody on the 1st Sunday of the month: Cluny, Picasso, Arts and Crafts, Orangerie, Orsay, Gustave Moreau Guimet, Quai Branly, History of Immigration, Centre Georges-Pompidou, City of Architecture and Heritage. Free Oct-March: the Rodin Museum. Free Nov-March: the Conciergerie, Sainte-Chapelle, Pantheon, Château de Versailles. The Louvre is free on the first Sat of the month from 6–9.45pm.

City of Paris museums

Free all year for their permanent collections (not for temporary exhibitions): Museum of the Romantics, the Cernuschi, Modern Art, Bourdelle and Zadkine Museums, the Petit Palais and Victor Hugo's house.

Museums at night

Free admission on Thursday to the Arts and Crafts Museum and certain others: check with the individual museums.

Open-air cinema

→ lavillette.com
Free screenings in the summer.

Personalized walks

→ greeters.paris
Visitors choose their language and explain their interests before being taken on a walk by a passionate local volunteer as a guide.

Auctions

→ 9, rue Drouot (9th)
drouot.com
Experience the workings of the Parisian art world by attending an auction in the Hotel Drouot (**C** F1).

Couscous

→ Le Grenier (**I** C1), 152, rue Oberkampf (11th); Les Trois Frères (**D** D3), 14, rue Léon (18th)
The owners of these two bars have found a way to attract customers… by offering free couscous on Thu night at Le Grenier, and on Fri and Sat at Les Trois Frères!

EASY ON THE WALLET

Paris Museum Pass

→ 2 days (€48), 4 days (€62), 6 days (€74)
parismuseumpass.com
Free entrance (and no waiting in line) to 50 museums and sites.

Passlib'

→ 2 days (€109), 3 days (€129), 5 days (€155)
parisinfo.com
Includes the Paris Museum Pass, as well as sightseeing tours and unlimited transport (zones 1–3).

Theater kiosks

→ 15, pl. de la Madeleine (8th) (**C** C2); pl. des Ternes (17th) (**E** D2); Esplanade Montparnasse (14th) (**G** B3)
Tue-Sat 12.30–2.30pm, 3–7.30pm; Sun 12.30–3.45pm (des Ternes is closed Tue and Sun)
Substantial discounts for tickets to most theater shows, on the same day as the performance

Kiosque jeunes

→ 10, passage de la Canopée, Forum des Halles (1st) (**B** B2)
Tue-Sat 11am–7pm
Free tickets and discounts to various shows for young people aged from 13 to 30.

Commercial theaters

→ theatresparisiens associes.com
Most commercial theaters offer €10 tickets to under 26-year-olds, only available at their box office.

Recycling centers

→ L'Alternative: 13, rue Léopold-Bellan (2nd) (**B** B1)
Tue-Sat 11am–7.30pm
→ La Petite Rockette: 125, rue du Chemin-Vert (11th) (**I** C1) Tue-Fri 1–7pm; Sat 11am–7pm
These ressourceries are governed by principles of sustainability and solidarity, which means that the pricing is fair.

Stock clearance/ thrift stores

Many brands sell their previous collections at knock-down prices: see Rues d'Alésia (**G** A4–C5), de Sévigné (**B** E3) and Beaurepaire (**J** A5). Thrift stores are plentiful in Le Marais (**B**).

OUTDOOR CINEMA IN LA VILLETTE

The city's neighborhoods

Each one with its own character and atmosphere...

The islands (A)
The islands on the Seine have formed the nucleus of Paris since the city's earliest days. In the third century the Île de la Cité served as the seat of political, judicial and religious power; now it is dominated by Notre-Dame. In its shadow, the Île Saint-Louis is marked out by its attractive alleys and quays.

Latin District (A)
Since the 13th century, this maze of narrow streets on the slopes of the Left Bank has been a student haunt; today's generation can still be found engaging in debates on the Saint-Geneviève Mountain and filling the arthouse cinemas in Saint-Michel... And why 'Latin'? Because it was the language of instruction in the university.

Saint-Germain-des-Prés (A)
In the post-war years, Sartre and Beauvoir would hold court in the Café de Flore, and Boris Vian would be a regular fixture in the jazz clubs. The literary spirit of Saint-Germain is still evident on its quiet streets, where bookshops and publishing houses hold their own against the big fashion and design labels.

Les Halles (B)
The old covered market has given way to the busy Forum shopping mall, although the bars on the Rue Montorgueil remain havens of peace.

Le Marais (B)
Originally marshland, this area was drained in the 13th century and later became a stronghold of high society. The mansion houses that lined the narrow streets have been joined by art galleries, thrift stores and trendy bars and shops. Le Marais is home to Europe's largest Jewish community, and there has also been a strong LGBTQ presence here since the 1980s.

Opéra/Grands Boulevards (C, D)
The area round the Opera House was once frequented by the aristocracy but it is now largely given over to cheap restaurants (including excellent Japanese ones on Rue Sainte-Anne.) Theaters and department stores attract crowds to the Grand Boulevards whilst various covered passageways offer a respite from the throng.

Montmartre (D)
The days of Montmartre's bohemian artists may be long gone but its steep alleyways bedecked with flowers have retained their charm.

Pigalle (D)
By day, hip barbershops, cafés and stores have made So-Pi (South of Pigalle) a paradigm of gentrification. Later, the nightlife more usually associated with the area takes over.

The West (E, F)
An elegant, picture-postcard area with luxury hotels, up-market restaurants, prestigious stores and embassies; and where limousines intermingle with the tourist buses around some of the city's iconic monuments.

Montparnasse (G)
The nerve center of the Parisian artistic community in the glory days of the 1920s still has thriving cinemas, theaters and brasseries.

Butte-aux-Cailles (H)
An altogether more provincial Paris, amidst the cosmopolitan patchwork of the 13th *arrondissement*. The walls of its cafés and former working-class houses have become a favorite canvas for street artists.

Bibliothèque/ Bercy (H, I)
These two neighborhoods on either side of the Seine have in common docks lined with barges for socialising; along with dramatic architectural transformation involving the conversion of former industrial premises and the creation of resolutely modern edifices.

The East (I, J)
Creative, cosmopolitan and down-to-earth, with lively bars in Oberkampf and around the Bastille. In Belleville are Asian and North African restaurants and stores, and green spaces alongside the canals and in the parks.

MÉNILMONTANT, EAST PARIS

Find your bearings in Paris

A Les Îles / Quartier Latin / Saint-Germain-des-Prés
B Les Halles / Le Marais
C Opéra / Louvre / Orsay
D Montmartre / Pigalle / Grands Boulevards
E Champs-Élysées / Batignolles

F Invalides / Tour Eiffel
G Montparnasse
H Butte-aux-Cailles / BnF / Bercy
I Bastille / Oberkampf / Nation
J Canal Saint-Martin / Belleville / Ménilmontant

SEINE

Porte de Clichy

E LA DÉFENSE

CITÉ JUDICIAIRE

Porte d'Asnières

Porte de Champerret

Porte de Champerret

BOULEVARD BERTHIER

XVI

BD COUVION ST-CYR

AVENUE DE WAGRAM

BOULEVARD

AVENUE DE VILLIERS

BD DE COURCELLES

PARC MONCEAU

MALESHE...

BELL... BATIG...

JARDIN D'ACCLIMATATION

FONDATION LOUIS-VUITTON

Porte Maillot

PALAIS DES CONGRÈS

AV. DE LA GRANDE-ARMÉE

ARC DE TRIOMPHE

AVENUE DE FRIEDLAND

BOULEVARD HAUSSMANN

PARC DE BAGATELLE

BOIS DE BOULOGNE ✪

BD DE L'AM.-BRUIX

Porte Dauphine

CHAMPS- ✪ ÉLYSÉES

AV. D'IÉNA

VIIIᵉ

PAL... DE L'ÉL...

BD LANNES

AVENUE VICTOR-HUGO

AV. H.-MARTIN AV. MANDEL

Porte de la Muette

PALAIS DE CHAILLOT

AV. KLÉBER

AV. DU-PDT.-WILSON

AVENUE MONTAIGNE

C. ALBERT-1er

GRAND PALAIS

C. LA-REIN...

SUCHET

XVIᵉ

JARDINS DU TROCADÉRO

AV. DE NEW YORK

SEINE

MUSÉE DU QUAI-BRANLY

QUAI D'ORSAY PA...

BOL...

JARDINS DU RANELAGH

Porte de Passy

MAISON DE RADIO-FRANCE

QUAI DE PASSY

AVENUE DE TOQUET

AVENUE DE LA BOURDONNAIS

EIFFEL ✪ TOWER

CHAMP- DE-MARS

HÔTEL DES INVALIDES

Place Vau...

V

BOULEVARD

A 13

Porte d'Auteuil

AV. DU PDT.-KENNEDY Q. DE GRENELLE

BD DE GRENELLE

AV. DE LA MOTTE-PIQUET

ÉCOLE MILITAIRE

U.N.E.S.C.O.

BD GARIBALDI

AV. DE BRETEUIL

AV. DES INVALIDES

R.DE...

JARDIN DES SERRES D'AUTEUIL

QUAI A-CITROËN

XVᵉ

BD EXELMANS

AVENUE DE VERSAILLES

PARC DES PRINCES

Porte de Saint-Cloud

PARC ANDRÉ-CITROËN

RUE LECOURBE

RUE DE VAUGIRARD

MONTPAR...

BD DU GÉN.-M-VALIN

BD VICTOR

Quai d'Issy

HÉLIPORT DE PARIS

Porte de Sèvres

PARC DES EXPOSITIONS

BD LEFEBVRE

PARC GEORGES BRASSENS

BOULEVARD

F

Porte de la Plaine

Porte de Brancion

Porte de Vanves

Porte de Châtillon

G

0   1   2 km
1/ 110 000 - 1 cm = 1,1 km

The Île de la Cité is the historic and geographic heart of Paris, filled with remnants of the old royal city. On the Rive Gauche (Left Bank) is the Latin Quarter with its art-house cinemas, small bars and universities. Further south, the 'Boul' Mich' (Boulevard St-Michel) climbs toward the Luxembourg Gardens, passing by the Sorbonne and the Rue Soufflot, which leads to the majestic Pantheon. To the west, the Place de l'Odéon has held on to its former elegance and the Rue St-André-des-Arts to its medieval alleyways. Nearby is St-Germain-des-Prés, with its postwar literary cafés and its chic boutiques.

LUISA MARIA   LES PAPILLES

RESTAURANTS

Cosí (B2) ¶❶¶
→ 54, rue de Seine (6th)
Tel. 01 46 33 35 36
Daily noon–11pm
Delicious oven-baked bread and the freshest of produce to spread on it such as tapenade, salmon and pickled tomatoes. Good wines. Set menu €11–14.

Luisa Maria (C3) ¶❷¶
→ 12, rue Monsieur-le-Prince (6th)
Tel. 01 43 29 62 49; Mon-Sat noon–2.30pm, 7.30–11pm
Contemporary, shabby-chic décor, with furniture from flea markets, this is the sister restaurant of Maria Luisa (2, rue Marie-et-Louise, ▐ A5). Delicious pasta and pizzas. Dishes €11–22.

Les Pipos (D3) ¶❸¶
→ 2, rue de l'École-Polytechnique (5th)
Tel. 01 43 54 11 40
Mon-Sat 9am–1am (kitchen open 11am–11pm)
On the pretty Mont Sainte-Geneviève, a traditional bistrot with plenty of character and communal tables to add to the conviviality. Dishes €12–18; set lunch menu €14.50.

Le Petit Saint-Benoît (B2) ¶❹¶
→ 4, rue St-Benoît (6th)
Tel. 01 42 60 27 92
Mon-Sat noon–2.30pm (3pm Sat), 6.30–10.30pm
A brasserie founded in 1901, run by the Gervais-Daffis family since 1960, where regulars keep their napkins in a tall cabinet with miniature drawers. Standard home cooking but the charm of a bygone age. Dishes €14–19.

Les Papilles (C4) ¶❺¶
→ 30, rue Gay-Lussac (5th)
Tel. 01 43 25 20 79; Tue-Sat noon–2pm, 7–10.30pm
Selected by the owner, who is from the south-west, an array of wines line the walls of this grocery-bistro. Charcuterie and traditional cuisine. Dishes €20–25 (lunch); set dinner menu €38.

Le Comptoir du Relais Saint-Germain (C2) ¶❻¶
→ 7, carrefour de l'Odéon (6th); Tel. 01 44 27 07 97
Mon-Fri noon–6pm, 8.30–11pm; Sat-Sun noon–11pm
The bistro of Yves Camdeborde, star of Parisian 'bistronomy', has a tiny dining room and a sidewalk terrace. Sample the brasserie menu (daytime and weekends) or a more elaborate dinner

PETITE VIENNOISE

CAVEAU DE LA HUCHETTE

VANESSA BRUNO

(weekdays; reserve). Try l'Avant-Comptoir de la Mer at no. 3, for aperitifs and more casual dining. Dishes €17–25; set menu €60 (dinner).

CAFÉS, BARS, CONCERTS

La Petite Viennoise (C3) 7
→ 8, rue de l'École-de-Médecine (6th)
Mon-Fri 8am–7.30pm
A tiny patisserie-tearoom: delicious strudels and Viennese hot chocolate, and a small selection of savory dishes for lunch.

Les Deux Magots (B2) 8
→ 6, pl. St-Germain-des-Prés (6th); Daily 7.30am–1am
Along with the Flore, 50 yards down (172, bd St-Germain), this is Paris's most famous literary café. Both were once the stronghold of Left Bank figures and existentialists: Picasso Hemingway, Sartre, De Beauvoir. A truly Parisian experience.

Café de la Mairie (B3) 9
→ 8, pl. St-Sulpice (6th)
Daily 7am (9am Sat-Sun)–11pm
Off the tourist track,

a café with a pleasant terrace opposite the church of St-Sulpice.

Prescription (B2) 10
→ 23, rue Mazarine (6th)
Tel. 09 50 35 72 87; Daily 7pm–2am (4am Fri-Sun)
Unusual cocktails (based on fresh fruit juice, marjoram, etc.) in this cozy bar. The same team runs L'Expérimental at 37, rue Saint Sauveur (B C1).

Chez Georges (B2) 11
→ 11, rue des Canettes (6th)
Tel. 01 43 26 79 15; Daily 6pm (3pm Sat)–2am
This typically St-Germain bar has remained unchanged since 1952. Come during the day for a game of chess or a glass of wine; in the evenings, students fill the cellar.

Le Piano Vache (D3) 12
→ 8, rue Laplace (5th)
Tel. 01 46 33 75 03
Mon-Fri noon–4pm, 7pm–2am; Sat 7pm–2am
On the Sainte-Geneviève mountain, this delightful old-fashioned bar has been defying the passage of time since 1969. Jazz manouche on Mondays; 1980s, blues, folk on other nights.

Caveau de la Huchette (D2) 13
→ 5, rue de la Huchette (5th)

Tel. 01 43 26 65 05; Daily 9pm–2am (4am Fri-Sat)
For the last 70 years this medieval cellar has been hosting jazz. Live music from 9.30pm; swing, blues and soul later.

SHOPPING

Berthillon (F3) 14
→ 29-31, rue St-Louis-en-l'Île (4th)
Tel. 01 43 54 31 61; Wed-Sun 10am–8pm (closed Aug)
The most celebrated ice-cream parlor in Paris is also a tearoom. Seven other outlets on the island on Mon-Tue in summer, when the main shop is closed.

Bookstalls (C2-E3) 15
→ Opening times vary according to the weather
These second-hand book stalls have stood on the banks of the Seine since the 19th century, filled with forgotten novels, old magazines, antique posters and cards.

Crocodisc (D3) 16
→ 40-42, rue des Écoles (5th); Tel. 01 43 54 33 22
Tue-Sat 11am–7pm
This second-hand record store has attracted music lovers since 1978: funk, reggae, US rap, world music and rock. Jazz and

blues at 64, rue de la Montagne-Sainte-Geneviève.

Pierre Hermé (B2) 17
→ 72, rue Bonaparte (6th)
Tel. 01 43 54 47 77; Daily 10am–7pm (8pm Fri-Sat)
Queues often form outside this patisserie, whose façade resembles a luxury jeweler. The biscuits, macarons and cakes of the 'Picasso of pastry', as Hermé is known, are sublime.

Fashion in Saint-Germain-des-Prés
The epicenter of Parisian chic and high-fashion.

Vanessa Bruno (B3) 18
→ 25, rue Saint-Sulpice (6th); Tel. 01 43 54 41 04; Mon-Sat 10am–7pm
Ultra-stylish womenswear.

Dona Giacometti (B3) 19
→ 6, rue Saint-Sulpice (6th)
Tel. 01 44 07 39 13
Mon-Tue, Thu-Sat 11am (2.30pm Mon)–7pm
Contemporary jewelry in glass, stone, gold and silver created by Dona herself in her boutique.

APC (A3) 20
→ 38, rue Madame (6th)
Tel. 01 42 22 12 77
Mon-Sat 11.30am–7.30pm
Raw denim jeans and jackets with simple, clean lines; the men's store is at no. 35.

The iron-framed pavilions built by Victor Baltard for Napoleon III to house the markets of the Halles are long gone; now crowds stroll under the majestic glass 'Canopée' that covers the vast shopping mall, the Forum. Nearby, the Centre Pompidou, with its forest of pipes, runs alongside the Stravinsky Fountain. On the other side of the rue de Rivoli, the square in front of the imposing Hôtel de Ville (City Hall) is a popular meeting place. To the east, on the winding streets of the Marais, splendid 17th-century town houses are ensconced behind imposing doors; and a succession of Jewish stores, fashion shops, art galleries and gay bars await visitors.

MIZNON

CHEZ JANOU

RESTAURANTS

Marché des Enfants-Rouges (E2) 🍴**❶**
→ 39, rue de Bretagne (3rd); Tue-Sun 9am-8pm (10.30pm Thu, 5pm Sun)
The oldest food market in Paris (1615) has tables to sit at to enjoy the produce and freshly made dishes from its stalls – sushi, tajines, pizza, salads. Dishes €5-15.

Miznon (D3) 🍴**❷**
→ 22, rue des Écouffes (4th); Tel. 01 42 74 83 58 Sun-Fri noon-11pm (3.30pm Fri)
Like its counterpart restaurant in Tel Aviv, great pitta bread filled with tasty meat or roasted vegetables with tahini sauce; and melted banana for the sweet version. Pitta €6.50-12.

Bistrot Beaubourg (C3) 🍴**❸**
→ 25, rue Quincampoix (4th); Daily noon-2am
A friendly, busy restaurant near the Pompidou Center serving simple but fresh and affordable food: andouillette, leeks in vinaigrette, etc. Dishes €7-20.

FTG (B1) 🍴**❹**
→ 9, rue du Nil (2nd) Tel. 01 40 26 23 43
Daily 8.30am-5pm
Next to Frenchie (at nos 5-6), this popular bar-restaurant ('Frenchie To Go') of the anglophile Grégory Marchand offers snacks including homemade pastrami sandwiches, 100% beef hot dogs and heavenly cookies. €8-22.

Café des Musées (E3) 🍴**❺**
→ 49, rue de Turenne (3rd) Tel. 01 42 72 96 17 Mon-Thu noon-2.30pm, 7-10.30pm; Fri-Sun noon-4pm, 7-11pm
The traditional, seasonal dishes served by this old-style bistro are highly prized so it is advisable to book. Andouillette, steak, homemade paté. Dishes €12-26; set lunch menu €21 (Mon-Fri).

Le Tambour (B1) 🍴**❻**
→ 41, rue Montmartre (2nd) Tel. 01 42 33 06 90 Daily 8.30am-5am (6am Thu-Sat)
A quirky bistro with a decor made up of road signs, fire hydrants and bygone métro maps. It feeds typical Parisian favorites (pigs' trotters, andouillette, steak tartare) to night owls. Dishes €14-23.

Chez Janou (F3) 🍴**❼**
→ 2, rue Roger-Verlomme

GAÎTÉ LYRIQUE

MA CAVE FLEURY

L'ÉCLAIR DE GÉNIE

(3rd); Daily 8am–2am (kitchen: noon–3pm (4pm Sat-Sun), 7pm–midnight) This Provençal bistro behind the Place des Vosges offers dishes from the south of France such as tuna carpaccio and fillet of sea bass. It gets busy, so while you're waiting for your table, relax with one of the 80 kinds of pastis on offer. There is a terrace. Dishes €19–25; set menu €16 (weekday lunch).

CAFÉS, BARS, ARTS VENUES

L'Ébouillanté (D4) **8**
→ 6, rue des Barres (4th)
March-Oct: Daily noon–10pm; Nov-Feb: Tue-Sun noon–7pm
Set in a pedestrianized street across from the church of St-Gervais-St-Protais. Ideal for lunch or tea on the terrace; brunch on Sundays.

Le Loir dans la Théière (E3) **9**
→ 3, rue des Rosiers (4th)
Daily 9am–7.30pm
(8pm Fri-Sat)
Sink into the comfortable, well-worn leather armchairs and linger for a while in this warm, busy tearoom. Delicious homemade cakes, tarts

and crumbles; salads at lunchtime.

Café noir (B1) **10**
→ 65, rue Montmartre (2nd)
Daily 8am (10am Sun)–2am
A splendid bar and an outdoor terrace make this small café a very pleasant spot. Le Cœur Fou, at no. 55, is also worth a visit.

L'Art brut (C2) **11**
→ 78, rue Quincampoix (3rd); Tel. 01 42 72 17 36
Daily 4pm–2am
Wrought-iron and wood decor, sculptures and large tables make up this warm and friendly bar: gypsy music, French songs, and cheap beer and brandy from the Balkans.

La Gaîté lyrique (C1) **12**
→ 3 bis, rue Papin (3rd)
Tue-Fri 2–10pm; Sat-Sun noon–10pm (6pm Sun)
A digital arts and modern music centre housed in a superb 19th-century theater: exhibitions, concerts, workshops, film screenings, talks.

Raymond Bar (B1) **13**
→ 13, rue Dussoubs (2nd)
Tue-Sat 6.30pm–2am
This former spa is now a fashionable bar but has kept its hammam (now a smoking room); music and a dancefloor.

SHOPPING

La Droguerie (B2) **14**
→ 9-11, rue du Jour (1st)
Tel. 01 45 08 93 27; Mon-Sat 10am (2pm Mon)–7pm
A haberdashery store with countless jars of beads and ribbons.

Ma Cave Fleury (C1) **15**
→ 177, rue Saint-Denis (2nd)
Tel. 01 40 28 03 39; Mon 5–10pm; Tue-Fri 11am–1pm, 5–10pm; Sat 11am–10pm
This 100% organic wine stockist sells the unique champagne of the Fleury family and wine from their producer friends. A glass of Champagne at reasonable prices in the evening and bites to eat.

French Trotters (E2) **16**
→ 128 rue Vieille-du-Temple (3rd); Tel. 01 44 61 00 14
Tue-Sat 11.30am–8pm; Sun 2–7pm
This fashionable brand sells its own off-the-peg clothes for men and women, as well as household items; also showcases work by designers worldwide.

Mariage Frères (D3) **17**
→ 30, rue du Bourg-Tibourg (4th); Tel. 01 42 72 28 11; Shop: Daily 10.30am–7.30pm; Tearoom:

Daily noon–7pm
A magnificent colonial-style shop packed with some 700 varieties of tea.

Sacha Finkelsztajn (D3) **18**
→ 27, rue des Rosiers (4th)
Tel. 01 42 72 78 91
Wed-Sun 10am–7pm
The best Jewish-Askhenazi deli in Paris: hummus, strudel, dill taramasalata, sernik (cheesecake) and bagels. Then if you like shopping, walk the Rue des Francs-Bourgeois, whose fashion shops are nearly all open on Sundays.

L'Éclair de Génie (E4) **19**
→ 14, rue Pavée (4th)
Tel. 01 42 77 85 11
Mon-Fri 11am–7pm; Sat-Sun 10am–7.30pm
Pastry chef Christophe Adam's éclairs are as delicious as they are beautiful: cocoa 'grand cru', salted caramel, vanilla-pecan and some more unusual flavors.

Izraël (D4) **20**
→ 30, rue François-Miron (4th); Tue-Sat 10am–1pm, 2–7pm
Be seduced by the scents of exotic spices in this store: tea from Mauritius, Indian curry, soap from Aleppo; also olives, rice and various delicacies.

Opéra / Louvre / Orsay

Facing one another across the river, the city's two greatest museums, the Louvre and Orsay, are firm favorites with tourists. Although the souvenir stores have invaded the arcades along the Rue de Rivoli, the area has lost none of its grandeur. Place de la Madeleine and the Rue Royale boast a number of designer tableware shops and luxurious delis; fashion designers line Rue St-Honoré; and Place Vendôme and Rue de la Paix are home to some of the most famous jewelry names in the world. To escape the noise of the streets, head for the peaceful gardens of the Palais-Royal, or its pleasant tearooms and elegant restaurants.

GRILLÉ

LE GRAND VÉFOUR

RESTAURANTS

Higuma (E2) 🍴❶
→ 32 bis, rue Ste-Anne (1st)
Daily 11.30am–10pm
On a street famous for its canteen-style Japanese eateries, diners eat at large tables while the chefs prepare ramen (noodle soup) and other dishes in sizzling woks. Also at 163, rue St-Honoré (C E3) and 27, bd des Italiens (C E1). Dishes €8–11; set menu €11–14.

Grillé (E2) 🍴❷
→ 15, rue St-Augustin (2nd) Tel. 01 42 96 10 64; Mon-Sat noon–4pm (9pm Wed-Sat)
This gastro kebab spot is supplied its meat by the Desnoyer butchers (G B4), and its bread is made on site. Kebab €9.

Le Petit Vendôme (D2) 🍴❸
→ 8, rue des Capucines (2nd); Tel. 01 42 61 05 88 Mon 8.30am–4.30pm; Tue-Sat 8am (10.30am Sat)–2am (kitchen: noon–3pm, 6.30–11.15pm)
This Auvergnat bistro serves grilled pigs' trotters, roasted chicken, tender beef strips, as well as its famous jambon-buerre. Great wine list and artisanal cheeses, too. Dishes €16–27; sandwich €5–8.

Willi's Wine Bar (E2) 🍴❹
→ 13, rue des Petits-Champs (1st); Tel. 01 42 61 05 09; Mon-Sat noon–midnight (kitchen closed from 2.30–7pm)
The wines collected by British wine expert Mark Williamson line the walls of this well-maintained bistro. Food made with local, fresh produce and a particularly heavenly dessert: black chocolate terrine with custard. Dishes €18–25; set menu €21 (lunch)–36.

Aux Lyonnais (E1) 🍴❺
→ 32, rue St-Marc (2nd) Tel. 01 42 96 65 04 Tue-Fri noon–2pm, 7.30–10pm; Sat 7–10pm
Alain Ducasse's bistro, in a splendid building dating from the end of the 19th century, specializes in Lyonnaise cuisine. Ancient recipes are revived for epicureans – traditional and heart warming. Dishes €24–34; set menu €28–35 (lunch).

Le Grand Véfour (E2) 🍴❻
→ 17, rue de Beaujolais (1st) Tel. 01 42 96 56 27; Mon-Fri 12.30–2pm, 8–10pm
One of the oldest and most famous

CAFÉ MARLY

ANGELINA

REPETTO

restaurants in Paris, set under the Palais-Royal arcades, with a listed decor, plush banquettes and three Michelin stars. Don't miss Guy Martin's now classic truffle-flavored foie gras ravioli. Reservations essential. Dishes €95–120; set menu €115 (lunch), €315 (dinner).

CAFÉS, BARS, CLUB

Le Café Marly (E3) **7**
→ *93, rue de Rivoli (1st)*
Daily 8am–2am
This stylish café and contemporary brasserie overlooks the glass pyramid and French sculpture rooms of the Louvre; coffee may be pricey but the views are majestic.

Angelina (D2) **8**
→ *226, rue de Rivoli (1st)*
Tel. 01 42 60 82 00; Mon-Fri 7.30am–7pm (7.30pm Fri); Sat-Sun 8.30am–7.30pm
Opened in 1903 under the arcades of Rue de Rivoli, this Viennese tea room, whose pastries are heavenly, also serves one of the best hot chocolates in Paris; it can also be taken out.

Bar de l'Entracte (E2) **9**
→ *47, rue de Montpensier*

(1st); *Mon-Sat 11.30am–3.30pm, 5.30pm–1am; Sun 2–8.30pm*
A historic café next to the Comédie-Française and Palais-Royal theaters, where actors and spectators alike share pre- or post-show drinks.

Truskel Microclub (F1) **10**
→ *12, rue Feydeau (2nd)*
Tel. 01 40 26 59 97
Tue-Sat 7pm–5am
Bottle-green windows, a wide choice of beers, football on the screens and rock music, this mini-club has DJs as well as live music and occasionally some after-hours gigs by cult bands.

Silencio (F2) **11**
→ *142, rue Montmartre (2nd); Tue-Thu 11pm–4am; Fri-Sat midnight–6am silencio-club.com*
Welcome to the world of David Lynch. The famous filmmaker dreamed up the decor for this select nightclub, which has acquired a reputation for eclectic and excellent programming.

Chez Carmen (F1) **12**
→ *53, rue Vivienne (2nd)*
Tel. 01 42 36 45 41
Tue-Sat midnight–7.30am (hours variable)
Night owls from all

around the city converge in this tiny bar for after-hours fun and frolics.

SHOPPING

Repetto (D2) **13**
→ *22, rue de la Paix (2nd)*
Mon-Sat 9.30am–7.30pm; Sun 11am–6pm
A legendary boutique well known by Opéra dancers and brought up to date by Issey Miyake. His ballet shoes come in an amazing range of colors and materials.

Françoise Montague (D2) **14**
→ *231, rue St-Honoré (1st)*
Tel. 01 42 60 80 16; Mon-Sat 10am (11am Sat)–7pm
Finely crafted jewelry made from resin, molten glass and crystal; custom pieces made to order. They sell vintage and costume jewelry, too.

Épicerie Roellinger (E2) **15**
→ *51 bis, rue Sainte-Anne (1st); Tel. 01 42 60 46 88*
Tue-Sat 10am–7pm
The Breton chef Olivier Roellinger shares his passion for spices in this deli whose shelves are filled with imaginative combinations.

Kitsuné (E2) **16**
→ *52, rue de Richelieu (1st)*
Mon-Sat 11am–7.30pm;

Sun 1–6.30pm
Kitsuné ('fox' in Japanese, hence the company logo) was founded by a French-Japanese duo to develop their shared interest in electronic music (via a record label) and fashion (via this elegant store).

The arcades of the Palais-Royal
The beautiful, romantic arcades are lined with high-fashion as well as old-fashioned boutiques.

Serge Lutens (E2) **17**
→ *142, gal. de Valois (1st)*
Tel. 01 49 27 09 09
Mon-Sat 11am–7pm
The exotic perfumes created by Serge Lutens for Shiseido are sold exclusively in this store.

Didier Ludot (E3) **18**
→ *18 and 24, gal. de Montpensier (1st)*
Tel. 01 42 96 06 56
Sep-June: Mon-Sat 11am–6.30pm;
July: Tue-Sat 11am–6.30pm
A treasure trove of a store containing Didier Ludot's collection of past Chanel and Dior creations, spanning forty years.

Anna Joliet (E2) **19**
→ *9, rue de Beaujolais (1st)*
Tel. 01 42 96 55 13
Mon-Sat noon–7pm
A doll's-house-style stall selling pretty music boxes.

High above the Abbesses district and its bars, the dazzling white domes and bell towers of the Sacré-Cœur Basilica draw the eye. The artists, cabarets and balls of the Belle Époque may be gone but the charm of Montmartre lives on in the steep streets, flights of steps and ivy-covered houses. On the boulevards at the foot of the Butte (mound) Montmartre, the clubs and venues fill up as evening falls on the gentrified Pigalle. Nearby is the 'Nouvelle Athènes' (New Athens) district, with its romantic streets lined with townhouses built in the 1820s – an oasis before the bustle of the Grand Boulevards.

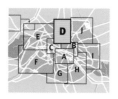

BOUILLON CHARTIER

LES PÂTES VIVANTES

RESTAURANTS

Pizza di Loretta (C5) 🍴❶
→ *43, rue La Fayette (9th)*
Tel. 01 44 63 33 51
Mon-Sat 11.30am–2.30pm,
8–10.30pm
Delicious pizzas with original toppings. Also at *62, rue Rodier* (C4). Priced by weight.

Bouillon Chartier (C6) 🍴❷
→ *7, rue du Fbg-Montmartre (9th); Tel. 01 47 70 86 29*
Daily 11.30am–midnight
A magnificent Belle Époque 'soup kitchen', and the first of its kind when it opened in 1896. It is touristy, the food is simple classic French – leeks in vinaigrette, endive salad with bacon – but it's fun. For a 21st-century version, try the Bouillon Pigalle, which unabashedly plays with the traditional formula (*22, bd. de Clichy; daily noon–midnight*). Dishes €8–13.

Au Bon Coin (B2) 🍴❸
→ *49, rue des Cloÿs (18th)*
Tel. 01 46 06 91 36; Mon-Sat 8am–midnight (kitchen: noon–3pm, 7–10.30pm)
On the far side of the Butte, away from the crowds, is a classic Parisian bistro with wines by the glass, charcuterie and brasserie-style food. Wine cellar next door. Dishes €9–14.

Les Pâtes Vivantes (C5) 🍴❹
→ *46, rue du Fbg-Montmartre (9th)*
Tel. 01 45 23 10 21; Daily noon–3pm, 7–11pm
A steamy, bustling Chinese cafeteria where fresh noodles (hence the name, 'noodles alive') are kneaded, stretched and hand-rolled in full view, then added to steaming bowls of soup with beef, tofu etc. Dishes €10–13.

Bien Élevé (C6) 🍴❺
→ *47, rue Richer (9th)*
Tel. 01 45 81 44 35
Tue-Fri noon–2pm, 7.30–9.30pm (10pm Fri); Sat 12.30–2pm, 7.30–10pm
The courteous service in this sophisticated restaurant with exposed stone walls is matched by the exquisite meat and fish, complemented by fresh, seasonal vegetables. Dishes €17–23; set lunch menu €19–36 (Mon-Fri).

Le Grand 8 (C3) 🍴❻
→ *8, rue Lamarck (18th)*
Tel. 01 42 55 04 55
Wed-Fri 7–10pm; Sat noon–2pm, 7–10pm
This little bistro is nestled on the Montmartre Hill,

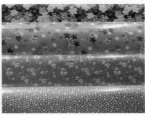

RENDEZ-VOUS DES AMIS   ANOUSCHKA   PETIT PAN

below Sacré-Coeur, and has lovley views of the city's rooftops. Traditional recipes using fresh, seasonal ingredients; natural wines.

CAFÉS, BARS, CLUB, MOVIE THEATER

Café Lomi (D3) **7**
→ 3 ter, rue Marcadet (18th)
Tel. 09 80 39 56 24
Mon-Fri 8am–6pm;
Sat-Sun 10am–7pm
This coffee-roasting house located in a loft serves Brazilian and African coffees with freshly made snacks and pastries. Tastings of different coffees.

Au Rendez-Vous des Amis (C4) **8**
→ 23, rue Gabrielle (18th)
Daily 9am–2am
A small, friendly café on the Butte but off the tourist track, popular with the locals.

La Fourmi (C4) **9**
→ 74, rue des Martyrs (18th)
Tel. 01 42 64 70 35; Mon-Fri 8am–2am (4am Fri); Sat 9am–4am; Sun 10am–2am
A few yards from the famous concert hall La Cigale, the Fourmi attracts the bright young crowds of the 18th arrondissement for

coffee, lunch or drinks.
Olympic Café (D3) **10**
→ 20, rue Léon (18th)
Tel. 01 42 59 97 09
Tue-Sat 5pm–2am
This perky bar in the Goutte-d'Or area hosts pop, rock and indie concerts downstairs.

La REcyclerie (C1) **11**
→ 83, bd Omano (18th)
Mon-Fri 8am–midnight (2am Fri); Sat noon–2am; Sun 11am–10pm
A former station on the Petite Ceinture rail track circling Paris has been converted into an organic café-bar-restaurant with an urban farm and a repair service for household goods. DJ sets.

Le Louxor (D4) **12**
→ 170, bd de Magenta (10th); Tel. 01 44 63 96 98
cinemalouxor.com
Now a listed building, this unusual movie theater (1921) with a neo-Egyptian-style decor has been restored to its former splendor. Three screens (for the decor choose no. 1) with an art-house programme. On the top floor is a bar and a terrace with a view onto the Sacré Coeur.

Le Dirty Dick (B4) **13**
→ 10, rue Frochot (9th)
Daily 6pm–2am (3am

Fri-Sat)
A trendy South of Pigalle crowd ensconces itself in this bar made out to look like a tropical beach: tiki masks, cocktails and punchy rhythms.

Rex Club (C6) **14**
→ 5, bd Poissonnière (2nd)
Tel. 01 42 36 10 96
Thu-Sat 11.30pm–7am (also certain Wednesdays)
Stalwart of the renowned nightlife scene of the Grand Boulevards, the Rex has, for more than 25 years, been one of the city's most important venues for electronic music – with some of the best DJs in the world.

SHOPPING

Anouschka (A5) **15**
→ 6, av. du Coq (9th)
Tel. 01 48 74 37 00
Mon-Fri noon–7pm by appt
Stylist Anouschka has organized her vintage finds chronologically, all by well-known designers.

Petit Pan (C4) **16**
→ 10 bis, rue Yvonne-Le Tac (18th)
Tel. 01 42 23 63 78
Daily 11am–1am, 2–7pm
Gorgeous mobiles, silk paper kites and colorful pajamas for children, all from China. Also at 76, rue

F.-Miron (**B** D4).
À la Mère de Famille (C6) **17**
→ 35, rue du Fbg-Montmartre (9th)
Tel. 01 47 70 83 69
Mon-Sat 9.30am–8pm;
Sun 10am–7.30pm
One of the last of its kind, this beautiful old-fashioned shop established in 1761 sells jams, sweets and candy: chocolate, calissons (sugar-coated almond paste), marrons glacés (candied chestnuts), etc. Also at 23, rue Lepic (**D** B4).

Marché Saint-Pierre (C4) **18**
→ 2, rue Charles-Nodier (18th); Tel. 01 46 06 92 25
Mon-Sat 10am–6.30pm (7pm Sat)
A truly wonderful fabric shop which has attracted sewing enthusiasts, designers and interior decorators for decades.

Guerrisol (C4) **19**
→ 17 bd de Rochechouart (9th)
Tel. 01 45 26 13 12; Mon-Thu, Sat 10.30am–7.30pm; Fri 10.30am–2pm, 3–7.30pm
Second-hand coats, T-shirts, shoes... Plunge into piles of clothes and find a bargain. In the same vein is Les stocks sympas at nos 66, 68 and 72.

Stretching majestically from La Concorde to the Arc de Triomphe, the Champs-Élysées is an unforgettable sight. The movie theaters, boutiques and clubs lining the famous avenue draw crowds day and night. To the south stand the Petit and Grand Palais, with the Alexandre III bridge (1900) beyond. To the north is the well-heeled 17th arrondissement, with the stunning Parc Monceau bordered by façades from the Haussmann period. The district recovers its bohemian spirit in the Rue des Dames and the Batignolles district. Towards Clichy, a disused railroad has become an ecological haven; and the new Palace of Justice by Renzo Piano towers over the city.

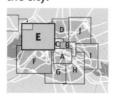

IRÈNE ET BERNARD

LE BAL CAFÉ OTTO

RESTAURANTS

Lucien la Chance (F2) ⑪
→ 8, rue des Dames (17th)
Tel. 09 73 52 07 14
Tue-Sat 6.30pm–1am
This small, convivial bistro specializes in small dishes that can be shared, tapas-style (foie gras, grilled sausage, matured cheese), as well as delicious desserts. Portions €7–12.

Irène et Bernard (F1) ②
→ 58, rue Gauthey (17th)
Tel. 01 42 29 56 16
Daily 8am (9am Sun)–2am
Kitchen: noon–11pm
(Sun 10pm)
This Batignolle spot, renovated in a traditional style, retains its bistro soul. Good brasserie dishes with homemade fries. Brunch Sat-Sun. Dishes €9–14.

Le BAL Café Otto (F2) ③
→ 6, impasse de la Défense (18th)
Tel. 01 44 70 75 51
Wed noon–10pm; Thu-Fri noon–7pm (10pm summer); Sat-Sun 11am–7pm
This new version of the stylish Café Otto serves tasty vegetarian dishes and mouthwatering pastries. Dishes €11–16; set lunch menu €18–22.

La Ripaille (F2) ④
→ 69, rue des Dames (17th)
Tel. 01 45 22 03 03
Mon-Fri noon–2pm,
7.30–10pm (10.30pm Fri)
Creative cuisine made from quality produce, amongst which wonderful fish and a Correze foie gras. Dishes €20; set lunch menu €12–20.

La Maison de l'Aubrac (D3) ⑤
→ 37, rue Marbeuf (8th)
Tel. 01 43 59 05 14
Daily noon–1am
(8am Wed-Sat)
'From the pitchfork to the fork' is this restaurant's motto. It specializes in beef, and the meat comes directly from owner Christian Valette's family farm. Traditional cuisine from the Aveyron region and a splendid wine list. Dishes €22–42.

Relais de Venise - L'Entrecôte (C2) ⑥
→ 271, bd Pereire (17th)
Tel. 01 45 74 27 97
Daily noon–2.30pm,
7–11.45pm
A brasserie next door to the Palais des Congrès, which since 1959 has been serving only one dish: a juicy sirloin steak with matchstick fries and

É JACQUEMART-ANDRÉ   LA PÂTISSERIE DES RÊVES   LES CAVES TAILLEVENT

their own secret sauce. No reservations: come either early or late if you don't want to wait. Dishes €28.

CAFÉS, BARS, CLUBS

Café Jacquemart-André (E3) 7
→ 158, bd Haussmann (8th)
Tel. 01 45 62 11 59
Daily 11.45am
(11am Sat-Sun)–5.30pm
(tearoom open from 3pm)
The elegant tearoom of the Jacquemart-André Museum, where you can sip tea beneath a ceiling painted by Tiepolo or have Sunday brunch on the terrace overlooking the garden.

Pasteleria Belém (F2) 8
→ 47, rue Boursault (17th)
Tel. 01 45 22 38 95
Tue-Sun 8am–8pm
An authentic Lisbon pâtisserie decorated with azulejos, and with only five tables. The pasteis de nata (small custard tart) is especially good.

3 Pièces Cuisine (F2) 9
→ 101, rue des Dames (17th)
Tel. 01 44 90 85 10
Mon-Fri 8.30am–2am
(1am Mon-Tue); Sat-Sun
9.30am–2am (1am Sun)

A homely, cosy café/bar opening onto the Rue des Dames offering good value burgers, salads and charcuterie and cheese plates. Ideal for aperitifs and for Sunday brunch.

Les Caves Populaires (F2) 10
→ 22, rue des Dames (17th)
Tel. 01 53 04 08 32
Daily 8.30am (10am
Sat, 11am Sun)–2am
Clashing with its trendy neighbours, a lively bar with no decor except for its chalk-boards displaying the bar's offerings of natural and organic wines.

Le Bistrot des Cinéastes (F2) 11
→ 7, av. de Clichy (17th)
Tel. 09 67 55 40 34
Daily 6pm–12.30am
Above an arty cinema which replaced the famous cabaret 'le Père Lathuille', a comfy hide-out in which to enjoy tapas.

Chez Raspoutine (D3) 12
→ 58, rue de Bessano (8th)
Tel. 01 47 20 02 90
Thu-Sat 11.30pm–5.30am
A glitzy Russian-themed nightclub, which is gloriously kitsch and attracts the gilded youth of Paris.

SHOPPING

Ladurée (F4) 13
→ 16, rue Royale (8th)
Tel. 01 42 60 21 79
Mon-Sat 8am–7.30pm (8pm
Fri-Sat); Sun 9am–7pm
A patisserie that could easily be a contender for the title of 'world's best macarons'. Around 20 flavors (including passion fruit, lavender and rose cardamom) served under kitsch Second Empire gildings. Other branches at 75, av. des Champs-Élysées (E D3) and 21, rue Bonaparte (A B2).

Batignolles organic market (F2) 14
→ Bd des Batignolles (between Rue Turin and Rue Puteaux); Sat 9am–3pm
A market selling organic fruit, vegetables, cheeses and other healthy specialties such as wheatgrass juice. The prices are high but so is the quality.

La Pâtisserie des Rêves (D2) 15
→ 19, rue Poncelet (17th)
Tel. 01 42 67 71 79; Tue-Fri
11am–7.30pm; Sat-Sun
9am–7.30pm (2pm Sun)
This patisserie creates beautiful pastries in the tradition of high French pastry making: Saint

Honorés, rum babas, calissons, éclairs...and their praline Paris-Brest is a dream. Also at 93, rue du Bac (G B1).

Les Caves Taillevent (D3) 16
→ 228, rue du Faubourg-St-Honoré (8th)
Tel. 01 45 61 14 09
Mon-Sat 10am–7.30pm
A famous cellar with more than 1,500 labels: everything from affordable wines from small vineyards to the rarest of grands crus.

Avenue Montaigne (D4) 17
The most prestigious names in haute couture line this avenue, among them Louis Vuitton at no. 22, Dior at no. 30, Nina Ricci at no. 39 and Chanel at no. 42.

Drugstore Publicis (D3) 18
→ 133, av. des Champs-Élysées (8th)
Tel. 01 44 43 75 07
Daily 8am (10am
Sat-Sun)–2am
This famous store is spread over two levels and has everything: international newspapers, stores, a pharmacy (open daily until 2am), a brasserie, wine cellar and cinema.

Ministries, embassies and other major institutions are the main occupants of the 7th arrondissement. Here too is the great gilded dome of the Invalides, whose classical outline dominates the vast esplanade. To the west is the École Militaire and the Champ de Mars, whose edges are bordered with fine town houses overlooking the Eiffel Tower. On the opposite bank, the stylish 1930s complex of the Trocadéro brings the fantastic view to a close. Further out, the 16th arrondissement is very grand in the north around the Avenue Foch, but more provincial in Passy and Auteuil.

AU DERNIER MÉTRO

CAFÉ CONSTANT

RESTAURANTS

Au Pied de fouet
(F2) 🍴**❶**
→ 45, rue de Babylone (7th)
Tel. 01 47 05 12 27; Mon-Sat noon–2.30pm, 7–11pm
A former coaching inn serving soup, steak, prunes poached in wine, etc. A small annex next door serves burgers and salads. Dishes €9–15.

Au Dernier Métro (D2) 🍴**❷**
→ 70, bd de Grenelle (15th)
Tel. 01 45 75 01 23
Daily 6.30am–2am (kitchen: 11am–1am)
Popular Basque bistro serving sausage with Espelette pepper, dishes *à la plancha* and other staples from the south west. Dishes €13–20.

Café de Mars (E2) 🍴**❸**
→ 11, rue Augereau (7th)
Tel. 01 45 50 10 90; Tue-Sat noon–2.30pm, 7.30–11pm
This retro-style bistro, on a small street near the Champs-de-Mars, stands out in this neighborhood by being neither too up-market nor a soulless eatery aimed at tourists. Seasonal produce. Dishes €18–21; set lunch menu €23–26.

Le Grand Pan (E4) 🍴**❹**
→ 20, rue Rosenwald (15th)

Tel. 01 42 50 02 50; Mon-Fri noon–2pm, 7.30–11pm
A popular neo-bistro where the meat is of exceptional quality and the natural wines are drawn from small càsks. Its younger brother, Le Petit Pan (at no. 18) has a bistrot menu in the day and serves tapas in the evenings. Dishes €14 (lunch), €18–32 (dinner).

Noura (E1) 🍴**❺**
→ 27, av. Marceau (16th)
Tel. 01 47 23 02 20
Daily 8.30am–midnight
One of the best Lebanese restaurants in Paris. 'Snack corner' if you're in a hurry, and the Noura deli across the road. Dishes €19–23.

Café Constant (E1) 🍴**❻**
→ 139, rue St-Dominique (7th); Tel. 01 47 53 73 34
Daily 7am (8am Sun)–11pm (kitchen: noon–5pm, 7–11pm)
More than just another neighborhood café. Modest prices for a Michelin-starred restaurant. Dishes €20–28; set lunch menu €21–27.

Le Chalet des îles (A1) 🍴**❼**
→ Bois de Boulogne, lower lake (16th); Tel. 01 42 88 04 69; April-Oct: Daily

NÉRAL BEURET

BOOK MARKET

LAURENT DUBOIS

noon–2.30pm, 7.30–11pm;
Nov–March: Wed–Sat
noon–2.30pm, 7.30–
10.30pm; Sun noon–3pm
A chalet perched on an
island in the middle of
the Bois de Boulogne,
given to the Empress
Eugénie by Napoleon.
Classic cuisine with a
modern twist, and some
Asian-inspired dishes.
Sunday brunch. Dishes
€20–36.

L'Ami Jean (E1) 🍴 **8**
→ 27, rue Malar (7th)
Tel. 01 47 05 86 89; Tue–Sat
noon–2pm, 7–11.30pm
A small bistro with
Basque memorabilia
and outstanding
seasonal cuisine. Dishes
€38–90; set menu €35
(lunch)–80 (dinner).

CAFÉS, BARS, MUSIC VENUES

Palais de Tokyo (D1) **9**
→ 13, av. du Président-
Wilson (16th)
Les Grands Verres: Daily
noon–2.30pm, 7–11pm
(bar: Daily 7pm–2am)
Monsieur Bleu: Daily
11am–2am; yoyo-paris.com
This imposing building
devoted to art is a
fashionable place to
meet: a long cocktail bar
and sophisticated

restaurant (Les Grands
Verres), a stylish
brasserie (Monsieur Bleu)
and an upmarket concert
hall and nightclub (Yoyo).
In summer, its esplanade
overlooking the Seine
serves as a terrace.

Carette (D1) **10**
→ 4, pl. du Trocadéro-et-
du-11-Novembre (16th)
Tel. 01 47 27 98 85; Daily 7am
(7.30am Sat–Sun)–11.30pm
A traditional tearoom
founded in 1927, popular
with the chic older ladies
of the *seizième*, who come
for brunch and Carette's
famous chocolate
macarons; snacks, too.

À la Petite Marquise (E2) **11**
→ 50, av. de La Motte-
Picquet; Tel. 01 47 34 94 03
Daily 7.30am–7.30pm
(lunch: noon–2.30pm)
A tearoom straight out
of the 1950s: leatherette
seats and coffee served
with petit fours, chocolate
ganaches, strawberry
shortbread biscuits...

Club des Poètes (F1) **12**
→ 30, rue de Bourgogne
(7th); Tel 01 47 05 06 03
Wed–Thu noon–2pm; Tue,
Fri–Sat noon–2pm, 8.30pm–
last customer
On Tuesday, Friday
and Saturday evenings
this small bar turns into a

poetry-lovers' hangout,
with some good vintages
to accompany the verse.

Rosa Bonheur sur Seine (F1) **13**
→ Quai d'Orsay (7th)
Tel. 01 47 53 66 92
June–Oct: Daily noon–
1.30am (midnight Mon–Tue)
Nov–May: Wed–Sun noon–
1.30am (midnight Sun)
The convivial, eccentric
spirit of Rosa Bonheur in
Buttes-Chaumont (J C4)
has been recaptured
onboard a barge which
has customers spilling
onto the quays.

Général Beuret (E3) **14**
→ 9, pl. du Général-Beuret
(15th); Tel. 01 42 50 28 62
Daily 8am–2am
A cheerful spot with a
terrace at the far end of
the 15th; the round zinc
bar is a museum piece.

Le Breguet (F3) **15**
→ 72, rue Falguière (15th)
Tel. 01 42 79 97 00
Mon–Sat 5pm
(6.30pm Sat)–1.30am
A lively bar where a
bunch of regulars (mostly
students) meet for drinks.

La Javelle B3 **16**
→ Port de Javel Bas (15th)
May–Sep: Daily noon–
midnight (weather
permitting)
On fine days, this stretch
of the river bank is

taken over by a modern
interpretation of a
guinguette (an open-air
dance hall): deckchairs,
yoga classes, street food
and night-time concerts
(*bal musette*, funk, salsa)
that get passersby
dancing.

SHOPPING

Davoli (E2) **17**
→ 34, rue Cler (7th)
Tel. 01 45 51 23 41
Tue, Thu–Sat 8.30am–
7.30pm; Sun 8.30am–1pm
A wonderful delicatessen:
Parma hams, Parmesan
cheese, vinegars, olive
oils and other delicacies.

Book market (E4) **18**
→ 104, rue Brancion (15th)
Sat–Sun 9am–6pm
Beneath the horse
market pavilion of
the former Vaugirard
slaughterhouses are
50 stalls selling second-
hand and rare books.

Laurent Dubois (D2) **19**
→ 2, rue de Lourmel (15th)
Tel. 01 45 78 70 58
Tue–Sun 9am (8.30am
Sat)–8pm (1pm Sun)
A renowned Parisian
cheesemonger, with
around 300 varieties
(which can be vacuum-
packed for traveling).

From the aristocratic Faubourg St-Germain, the boutique-lined Rue du Cherche-Midi and Rue du Bac lead down to Montparnasse and its tower, which is under renovation. Around the Vavin intersection are several cozy cafés and Art Deco brasseries, a legacy from the Belle Époque, when this was the bohemian and artistic nerve center of the city. Beyond the Montparnasse Cemetery are the Place Denfert-Rochereau, with its replica of Bartholdi's famous Lion of Belfort, and the pedestrian Rue Daguerre. To the south, the 14th arrondissement extends down to the pretty Parc Montsouris, and is dotted with gastronomic bistros.

TI JOS

LES PETITS PLATS

RESTAURANTS

Ti Jos (B3) ❶
→ 30, rue Delambre (14th)
Mon-Sat noon–2.30pm,
7–11pm (Sat 11.30pm)
One of the best Breton crêperies in the area (since 1937). Buckwheat savory pancakes, cider and Breizh cola. Crêpes €4–10.

Enzo (B4) ❷
→ 72, rue Daguerre (14th)
Tel. 01 43 21 66 66; Mon-Sat noon–2.30pm, 7–10.30pm
Enzo's trattoria only has room for a few tables so reserve ahead. Good pasta dishes and great pizzas (also to take out). Dishes €10–18.

Les Petits Plats (B5) ❸
→ 39, rue des Plantes (14th)
Tel. 01 45 42 50 52
Mon-Sat noon–2pm,
7.30–10pm
This Michelin-starred bistro has retained its 1910 atmosphere with mirrors and mouldings. It offers small taster plates as well as standard-size dishes: fish tartare, meat from the Aubrac. Dishes €15–26; set lunch menu €18–45.

La Cabane à huîtres (B2) ❹
→ 4, rue Antoine-Bourdelle (15th)
Tel. 01 45 49 47 27; Wed-Sat noon–2.15pm, 7–10.15pm
A tiny eatery of the type usually found in the southwest of France. It belongs to Francis Dubourg, oyster farmer and restaurateur. Try his traditionally cultivated oysters (or foie gras, or smoked duck breast). Set menu €23–31.

La Cantine du Troquet (A4) ❺
→ 101, rue de l'Ouest (14th)
Tel. 01 45 40 04 98
Tue-Sat noon–2.30pm,
7–10.45pm
No reservations here, so arrive early to this boho-chic cafeteria for fish à la plancha, black pudding pie, rice pudding and other retro bistro dishes. Dishes €19–24; set menu €35.

L'Assiette (B4) ❻
→ 181, rue du Château (14th); Tel. 01 43 22 64 86
Wed-Sun noon–2.30pm,
7.30–10.30pm
The chef here, David Rathgeber, who was trained by the famous Alain Ducasse, brings excellence to traditional cooking: quenelle of zander, calf's head, crème caramel. Dishes €25–39; set lunch menu €23.

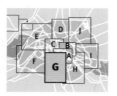

CHERCHEMINIPPES

LA GRANDE ÉPICERIE DE PARIS

CAFÉS, BARS

Café Tournesol
(B3) **7**
→ 9, rue de la Gaîté (14th)
Daily 8.30am–2.30am
A friendly café amidst the theaters and sex shops of the Rue de la Gaîté, with outdoor seating and a lively atmosphere.

La Coupole (B3) **8**
→ 102, bd du Montparnasse (14th)
Daily 8am–midnight (11pm Sun, Mon)
A Parisian landmark. The bohemian spirit of the 1930s has long gone, but the bar/brasserie still cuts a fine figure with its 33 pillars and Art Deco furniture.

Shannon Pub (C2) **9**
→ 23, rue Bréa (6th)
Tel. 01 43 26 34 70; Daily 6pm (7pm Sun)–4.30am
An Irish-style pub where the drinking and dancing go on until the early hours.

La Closerie des Lilas (C3) **10**
→ 171, bd du Montparnasse (6th); Tel. 01 40 51 34 50
Daily 11am–1.30am
Gide, Hemingway, Lenin, Beckett...each has a gold plaque commemorating his presence in this legendary brasserie that started out as a coaching

inn in the late 19th century and went on to draw all manner of literary and creative spirits from around the world; piano bar and secluded terrace.

MOVIE THEATERS, ARTS VENUES

Lucernaire (C2) **11**
→ 53, rue Notre-Dame-des-Champs (6th)
Tel. 01 45 44 57 34; Daily 10.30am–1am (10pm Sun)
A dynamic arts venue at the heart of the student quarter that surrounds the Rue Vavin. It is home to live theater, photo exhibitions and art-house and experimental movies. There's also an inexpensive restaurant and a quirky bar with a terrace on the street.

Lieu secret L'Entrepôt
(A4) **12**
→ 7-9, rue F.-de-Pressensé (14th)
Tel. 01 45 40 07 50
lentrepot.fr
This cultural powerhouse, which opened in an old printshop in 1975, has received a facelift and taken on new functions. While still serving as a cinema, it has now acquired a bar-restaurant (Simon Horowitz) with a shady garden and an

auditorium with an eclectic program of live performances.

SHOPPING

Chercheminippes
(B2) **13**
→ 102, rue du Cherche-Midi (6th); Tel. 01 45 44 97 96
Mon-Sat 11am–7pm
Six second-hand clothes stores on this elegant street: women's fashion at nos 109 and 114, homeware at no. 106, accessories and childrenswear at no. 110, menwear at no. 111 and youthwear at no. 124.

Le Bon Marché
(B1) **14**
→ 24, rue de Sèvres (7th)
Tel. 01 44 39 80 00
Mon-Sat 10am–8pm (8.45pm Thu); Sun 11am–7.45pm
Pioneer of department stores (1887) founded by Aristide Boucicaut, and for which Gustave Eiffel created the framework.

La Grande Épicerie de Paris **15**
→ 38, rue de Sèvres (7th)
Tel. 01 44 39 81 00
Mon-Sat 8.30am–9pm; Sun 10am–8pm
A terrific deli selling quality produce from around the world (Asian, Italian, Indian, Greek,

Spanish...) as well as champagnes, ciders, beers and wine.

Sonia Rykiel (B4) **16**
→ 112, rue d'Alésia (14th)
Tel. 01 45 43 80 86
Mon-Sat 10.30am (noon Mon)–7pm
The fashion designer Sonia Rykiel's striking creations stand out in this street known for its discount stores.

Boucherie Hugo Desnoyer (B4) **17**
→ 45, rue Boulard (14th)
Tel. 01 45 40 76 67
Tue-Fri 7am–1pm, 4-7.30pm; Sat 7am–5pm
One of the best butcher's shops in Paris and the supplier to some of the city's top restaurants: milk-fed veal, Salers beef, etc.

P. Boursault (B5) **18**
→ 71, av. du Général-Leclerc (14th)
Tel. 01 43 27 93 30
Tue-Fri 9am–1pm, 3.30–7.30pm; Sat-Sun 9am–7.30pm (1pm Sun)
Over 250 varieties of cheese, including the hard-to-find Termignon blue, as well as camemberts with Calvados and Époisses ripen slowly in the cellars. A vacuum-packing service is available.

The busy streets of the Mouffetard district lie beyond the Jardin des Plantes and the Grande Mosquée. From there the Avenue des Gobelins leads to the Place d'Italie, the heart of the 13th arrondissement. Nearby is the former village of the Butte-aux-Cailles, and out toward the Porte de Choisy is the Parisian Chinatown (1970). The eastern edge is bordered by the Seine and the old industrial wastelands of Bercy and Austerlitz, which are now home to the Cité de la Mode et du Design, the university hub of the Grands-Moulins and the BNF (Bibliothèque Nationale de France), at the foot of which the party barges are moored.

LAO LANE XANG

L'OURCINE

RESTAURANTS

La Felicità (C4) ¶❶│
→ Station f, parvis Alan-Turing (13th); Mon-Tue 12.15–3.30pm; Wed-Fri 12.15–2.30pm, 6–10.30pm (11pm Thu-Fri); Sat-Sun noon–11pm (10.30pm Sun)
The Freyssinet covered market houses an enormous Italian restaurant capable of seating 1,000 customers, opened by the enterprising Big Mamma group (fresh pasta, pizzas, ice creams). Its terrace is huge, while the interior decor includes two converted train wagons. Dishes 8–16€.

Chez Gladines (A4) ¶❷│
→ 30, rue des Cinq-Diamants (13th) Tel. 01 45 80 70 10 Sun-Thu noon–3pm (4pm Sun); Fri-Sat noon–3pm (4pm Sat), 7pm–1am
An informal Basque restaurant that gets very busy. Generous salads and tasty specialties from the South West. Good value for money. Dishes €9–15.

Lao Lane Xang (B5) ¶❸│
→ 105, av. d'Ivry (13th) Tel. 01 45 85 19 23 Tue-Sun noon–3pm, 7–11pm (10.30pm Sun)
This large restaurant focuses on spicy dishes from the Mekong Delta (Laos, Vietnam, Thailand): bo bun, shrimps sautéed with basil...Dishes €9–24; set lunch menu (Mon-Fri) €12.80.

Li Ka Fo (B5) ¶❹│
→ 39, av. de Choisy (13th) Tel. 01 45 84 20 45 Daily noon–midnight
In the Asian 13th arrondissement, this Cantonese restaurant serves tasty dishes in generous portions. Dishes €8–13.

Le Temps des Cerises (A5) ¶❺│
→ 18-20, rue de la Butte-aux-Cailles (13th) Tel. 01 45 89 69 48; Mon-Sat noon–2.30pm, 7–11.30pm
A workers' cooperative opened in 1976 – relaxed and still a bit libertarian. Hearty home cooking: Normandy-style black pudding, braised pork cheek. Dishes €13–21; set menu €14–16 (lunch), €21–26 (dinner).

Les Délices d'Aphrodite (A3) ¶❻│
→ 4, rue de Candolle (5th) Tel. 01 43 31 40 39 Daily noon–2.15pm, 7–11pm
The gourmet taverna of the Mavrommátis brothers: great moussaka

TEAROOM OF THE GRANDE MOSQUÉE   CITÉ DE LA MODE ET DU DESIGN / WANDERLUST   LES ABEILLES

and superb meze. Dishes €19–28; set lunch menu €23–25.

L'Ourcine (A3) **7**
→ 92, rue Broca (13th)
Tel. 01 47 07 13 65; Tue-Sat noon–2pm, 7.30–10.30pm
Sylvain Daniere learned his trade under the formidable Yves Camdeborde at La Régalade, and now runs his own restaurant with obvious passion, inspired by seasonal produce and working directly with small wine producers. Exceptional cuisine. Reservation advised. Set menu €28–38.

TEAROOMS, CAFÉS, BARS, CLUBS

Tearoom of the Grande Mosquée (A2) **8**
→ 39, rue Geoffroy-St-Hilaire (5th)
Tel. 01 43 31 38 20; Daily 9am–midnight (restaurant: noon–3.30pm, 7–11.30pm)
Small tables in the courtyard under the olive trees, a Moorish interior and sofas inside the mosque. Tagines, crunchy honey-soaked baklavas, mint tea…

Les 400 Coups (D3) **9**
→ 51, rue de Bercy (12th)
Wed-Mon 11am–8.30pm (10pm Sat, 7pm Sun)

The café of the Cinémathèque Française (on the ground floor) opens onto the lawns of the Parc de Bercy. Organic wines, artisanal beers and snacks; brunch on Sundays. Kid-friendly.

L'Âge d'Or (B5) **10**
→ 26, rue du Dr Magnan (13th); Tel. 01 45 85 10 58
Mon-Fri 9am–midnight (2am Thu-Fri); Sat noon–2am; Sun 10am–midnight
A unique bar-restaurant that runs workshops for children and adults, and hosts concerts.

La Folie en Tête (A5) **11**
→ 33, rue de la Butte-aux-Cailles (13th)
Mon-Sat 5pm–2am
A laid-back café in the old village of Butte-aux-Cailles, imaginatively decorated with wooden musical instruments from all over the world.

Le Merle Moqueur (A5) **12**
→ 11, rue de la Butte-aux-Cailles (13th); Daily 5pm–2am
An institution on the Butte, this buzzing, friendly bar is always packed; music from the 1970s–2000.

Cité de la mode et du Design (C3) **13**
→ 32–36, quai d'Austerlitz (13th); Rooftop: Mon-Sat

2pm–5am; Sun noon–midnight (Fri-Sat 10pm–5am in winter) Wanderlust: Tue-Sun 6pm–6am (Fri-Sat 11pm–6am in winter)
The Cité de la mode et du Design has quickly become one of the hubs of Parisian nightlife. Its rooftop and immense terrace facing the Seine are the most prized areas. On the ground floor (on the south side) is the bar-club Wanderlust, which also has a huge terrace.

Barges by the National Library (C3-D4) **14**
→ Quais de la Gare and quai F.-Mauriac (13th)
A flotilla of barges for partying are moored at the foot of the Bibliothèque François-Mitterand. In summer, their terraces spill over onto the docks.

Petit Bain (D4)
→ Tel. 01 43 49 68 92
Cafeteria and rooftop: Tue-Sun 6pm–midnight (2am Fri-Sat) Club: Fri-Sat midnight–6am
All areas of this delightful barge are imaginatively put to use, from the bridge to the hold: a bar, a cafeteria and a club, with a varied program.

La Dame de Canton (D4)

→ Opposite 11, quai F. Mauriac (13th)
Tel. 01 53 61 08 49
Tue-Thu 7pm–midnight; Fri-Sat 7pm–2am (5am if a DJ is playing)
Authentic wooden junk boat that hosts concerts (vocal, rock, funk, pop and world music) and sometimes has a DJ.

SHOPPING

Paris Jazz Corner (A2) **15**
→ 5, rue de Navarre (5th)
Tel. 01 43 36 78 92
Tue-Sat noon–8pm
More than 40,000 CDs and LPs covering the history of jazz, blues and gospel.

Les Abeilles (A5) **16**
→ 21, rue de la Butte-aux-Cailles (13th)
Tel. 01 45 81 43 48
Tue-Sat 11am–7pm
The small shop of a Parisian beekeeper, whose bees work in the 13th arrondissement. Also stocks honey from around the world.

Tang Frères (B5) **17**
→ 44, av. d'Ivry (13th)
Tel 01 45 70 80 00
Mon-Sat 9.30am–8pm
An Asian supermarket with an amazing range of products. Another store at no. 48.

CHEZALINE

SEPTIME

Place de la Bastille is where the capital's dedicated nightlife starts. Cafés and restaurants line the surrounding streets: de la Roquette, de Lappe, and de Charonne. But push on further east along the Rue du Faubourg-St-Antoine to discover a maze of courtyards and passageways. Cabinet-makers, for whom this area is renowned, still work here, now alongside designers, architects, graphic designers and stylists. To the north, the Oberkampf area has long been known for its alternative bars and in-vogue hangouts. Eastwards is the famous 109-acre Père-Lachaise cemetery.

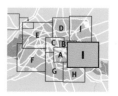

RESTAURANTS

CheZaline (C2) ⌖❶
→ 85, rue de la Roquette (11th); Tel. 01 43 71 90 75
Mon-Fri 11.30am–4pm
Delphine Zampetti's snack and lunch-box bar is one of the best in Paris: sandwiches, salads, homemade terrines and desserts. Snacks €5–9; daily special €10.

Little Hanoi (D2) ⌖❷
→ 9, rue de Mont-Louis (11th); Tel. 01 46 59 01 40
Daily noon–2.30pm, 7–10.30pm
The younger brother of the famous Vietnamese diner Paris Hanoi (74, rue de Charonne, I C3) is a more spacious affair. Wonderfully fresh food and terrific bò bún. Dishes €10–13.

Jacques Mélac (D2) ⌖❸
→ 42, rue Léon-Frot (11th) Tel. 01 43 70 59 27
Tue-Sat noon–3pm, 7–11pm
Vines cover the façade of Chez Mélac, where you can find saucisse sèche from the Aveyron region, cheese from Cantal and good house specials. Dishes €15–22; set menu €15.

Soya (B1) ⌖❹
→ 20, rue de la Pierre-Levée (11th); Tel. 01 48 06 33 02
Tue 7–11pm; Wed-Sat noon–3.30pm, 7–11pm; Sun 11.30am–3.30pm
Healthy, 100% vegan cooking: lasagne, mezze, couscous, and a popular brunch on weekends. Dishes €16–20; set lunch menu €15–23.

Mansouria (C3) ⌖❺
→ 11, rue Faidherbe (11th) Tel. 01 43 71 00 16
Mon 7.30–10.30pm; Tue-Sat noon–2.30pm, 7.30–10.45pm
This renowned Moroccan restaurant, run by Fatéma Hal, serves exceptional couscous and tajines. Also offers a catering service. Dishes €17–26; set menu €28–34.

Chateaubriand (B1) ⌖❻
→ 129, av. Parmentier (11th) Tel. 01 43 57 45 95
Tue-Sat 7–11pm
One of the best neo-bistro tables in town, belonging to Basque chef Inaki Aizpitarte. His daily-changing menu combines unlikely flavors – foie gras in miso soup, teriyaki salmon with berries and beetroot. At no. 131 is Aizpitarte's tapas bar, Le Dauphin. Set menu €75.

Septime (C2) ⌖❼
→ 80, rue de Charonne (11th); Tel. 01 43 67 38 29

INTERNATIONAL

LA BAGUE DE KENZA

L'AUTO-ÉCOLE

Mon 7.30–10pm; Tue-Fri 12.15–2pm, 7.30–10pm
A rustic-contemporary décor for this restaurant where the chef Bertrand Grébaut creates quality, modern and inspired cuisine. Reserve. Set menu €42–70 (lunch), €80–135 (dinner).

CAFÉS, BARS, CLUBS

Le Baron Rouge (C3) **8**
→ 1, rue Theophile-Roussel (12th); Tel 01 43 43 14 32
Mon 5–10pm; Tue-Fri 10am–2pm, 5–10pm; Sat-Sun 10am–10pm (4pm Sun)
A wine bar frequented by the locals when the Aligre market is in full swing, with wines from the cask, oysters (weekends from Sep-April), cheeses and charcuterie.

Pure Café (C2) **9**
→ 14, rue Jean-Macé (11th)
Tel 01 43 71 47 22
Mon-Sat 7am (8am Sat)–1am; Sun 9am–midnight
Away from the action is this charming bar (1920) with a zinc counter and luminous dining room.

Mama Shelter (E2) **10**
→ 109, rue de Bagnolet

(20th); Tel. 01 43 48 45 45
Daily 7am–1.30am
Ultra sleek and chic, the decor here by Philippe Starck) evokes a New York loft. There is a restaurant, a bar, a pizzeria and two terraces (one on the roof). Simple, quality dishes and Sunday brunch.

Le Perchoir (C1) **11**
→ 14, rue Crespin-du-Gast (11th)
Tel. 01 48 06 18 48
Daily 6pm (4pm Fri, 2pm Sat-Sun)–2am (Wed-Sat 6pm–2am in winter)
Sample a cocktail overlooking Paris, from the 7th floor bar of this otherwise unassuming building.

Le Balajo (B2) **12**
→ 9, rue de Lappe (11th)
Tel. 01 47 00 07 87
Mon 2–7pm; Tue-Thu 7.30pm–2am (dawn Thu); Fri-Sun 11pm–dawn
Opened in 1936, the 'Bal à Jo' revives the tradition of the afternoon dance (Mon), with live accordion music. Evening classes: salsa (Tue, Thu), rock 'n' roll (Wed). Club nights (Thu-Sat).

L'International (C1) **13**
→ 5-7, rue Moret (11th)
Tue-Sat 7pm–2am

(6am Fri-Sat)
A large, relaxed bar with back-to-back concerts in the basement: hip-hop, rock and electro music.

Ground Control (C3) **14**
→ 81, rue du Charolais (12th); Wed-Fri noon–midnight; Sat-Sun 11am–midnight (10pm Sun)
A cultural collective is temporarily running premises formerly operated by the French railroad company. The motto is 'Free and Curious': a terrace, dining room, bar (set inside an airplane!), an orchard, markets, art galleries, workshops…

SHOPPING

Isabel Marant (B3) **15**
→ 16, rue de Charonne (11th)
Tel. 01 49 29 71 55
Mon 11am–7pm;
Tue-Sat 10.30am–7.30pm
One of five outlets for this French fashion designer who combines elegance with originality in ethnic-inspired modern designs.

Gaëlle Barré (C2) **16**
→ 17, rue Keller (11th)
Tel. 01 43 14 63 02
Tue-Sat 11am–7.30pm
In her workshop-boutique, Gaëlle offers

retro fashion that is both romantic and feminine – distinguished by their beautiful fabrics and gorgeous prints.

Merci (B2) **17**
→ 111, bd Beaumarchais (3rd); Tel. 01 42 77 00 33
Mon-Sat 10am–7.30pm
A chic, ethical concept-store selling clothes, second-hand and designer furniture. Part of the profits go to charity. Two cafés.

La Bague de Kenza (C1) **18**
→ 106, rue St-Maur (11th)
Tel. 01 43 14 93 15
Sat-Thu 9am–9pm;
Fri 2.30–9pm
The best Algerian tearoom-patisserie in Paris has a wide choice of delicately flavored cakes (baklavas, 'gazelle horns'…) and savory specialties. Also at 173, rue du Fbg-St-Antoine (I C3).

L'Auto-École (C1) **19**
→ 101, rue Oberkampf (11th); Tel. 01 43 55 31 94
Mon 2–8pm; Tue-Sat 11am–2pm, 2.30–8pm
A colorful bric-a-brac of a store filled with toys, costume jewelry, bags, clothes, accessories, stationery, gift items, etc. at reasonable prices.

Canal Saint-Martin / Belleville / Ménilmontant

Along the canals, Paris past and Paris present stand side by side. The Canal St-Martin is full of old-fashioned charm, whilst hip boutiques and cafés abound on its banks. The Canal de l'Ourcq continues as far as La Villette, a thoroughly 20th-century 'garden city' that suddenly appears out of nowhere. Further south, the Parc des Buttes-Chaumont, renovated in 1864 to regenerate the surrounding slum area, has given birth to a respectable residential district. Below it are the old working-class villages of Belleville and Ménilmontant, with new Asian and North African influences and a busy market on Boulevard de Belleville.

LE VIEUX BELLEVILLE

LE VERRE VOLÉ

RESTAURANTS

Lao Siam (C5) ❶
→ 49, rue de Belleville (19th); Tel. 01 40 40 09 68
Daily noon–3pm, 7–11.30pm
People in the know all agree that Lao Siam serves some of the best Thai food in Paris, delicately scented with spices, basil, ginger, coconut and lemongrass. Dishes €9–22.

Mon Oncle le Vigneron (C4) ❷
→ 71, rue Rébeval (19th) Tel. 01 42 00 43 30; Mon-Sat 11am–2.30pm, 6–10pm
A restaurant-deli run by a friendly Franco-Japanese couple, selling good wines from small vineyards, regional produce and a freshly made dish of the day. Reserve for dinner. Dishes €11–13 (lunch); set dinner menu €24–29.

Le Vieux Belleville (C5) ❸
→ 12, rue des Envierges (20th); Tel. 01 44 62 92 66
Mon, Wed 11am–3pm; Tue, Thu-Fri 11am–3pm, 7.30pm–2am (midnight Tue); Sat 7.30pm–2am
Traditional in the best sense of the word, with old Parisian posters on the walls and Piaf or Arletty songs to sing along to in the evenings. Traditional cuisine such as steak in pepper sauce. Dishes €16–22.

Ohinéné (D5) ❹
→ 14, rue de la Chine (20th) Tel. 01 71 20 67 62
Mon 11.30am–2.30pm; Tue-Sat 11am–2.30pm, 7.30–10pm
An Ivory Coast restaurant where the banana crisps, grilled meats and creative desserts charm the locals. Dishes €12.50 (lunch), €17–25 (dinner); set menu €18 (lunch).

Le Verre Volé (A5) ❺
→ 67, rue de Lancry (10th) Tel. 01 48 03 17 34
Daily 12.30–2pm, 7.30–10.30pm
This pioneer of bistro-wine bars is still going strong. Excellent wine list and good French cuisine. Dishes €16–29.

Quedubon (C4) ❻
→ 22, rue du Plateau (19th) Tel. 01 42 38 18 65
Tue-Fri noon–2pm, 7.30–10.30pm; Sat 7.30–10.30pm
This restaurant-wine bar is well named (que du bon means 'nothing but good') and prides itself on naturally produced wines and homemade cooking. Dishes €17–34; set lunch menu €15–18.

the Hôtel de Donon, now the Cognacq-Jay Museum (*see box*), showcases 18th-century art, while the Hôtel Salé houses the Picasso Museum (**B** E3). After this cultural immersion, pass through the austere entrance of the National Archives on the Rue des Quatre-Fils, which leads to the surprising garden of the Hôtel de Soubise (**B** D3), one of the many tucked away in the backstreets of Le Marais.

From the Hôtel de Soubise to the Rue des Archives

The Rue des Francs-Bourgeois is renowned for its clothes stores, which are unusual in Paris for opening on Sundays. Fashion fans are equally in their element on the Rue Vieille-du-Temple, and the narrow side street, the Rue de Sévigné. The Rue de Thorigny specializes in contemporary art, and has a number of enterprising galleries. Not far away, the Place des Vosges (**B** E4) is noted for its harmonious architecture, particularly its arcades, which have become a popular meeting point. Victor Hugo lived here for many years, on the 2nd floor at no. 6, and his house is now open to the public (*see box*). Rue Saint-Antoine has an architectural delight too: the magnificent façade of the Hôtel de Sully (**B** E4). A stone's throw away, Garrice (*see box*) is a top-end store for women's footwear. Continue the walk in the peaceful alleyways of the Saint-Paul neighborhood, which has an abundance of antique shops. Other attractions here include the Gothic arabesques of the Hôtel de Sens and the photographic exhibitions put on by the MEP (**B** D4). Stop for a drink on the terrace of L'Ébouillanté (**B** D4), opposite the beautiful Church of Saint-Gervais-Saint-Protais, before diving into the heart of the Pletzl ('small square' in Yiddish) or Jewish neighborhood: the Rue des Rosiers is lined with Kosher falafel restaurants and Ashkenazi grocery shops. The atmosphere changes once again on the route down the Rue Vieille-du-Temple to the Rue des Archives, as this area is the epicenter of gay nightlife; and the terrace of the Open Café (*see box*) is lively from early evening onward.

🍴 Café Ineko
→ 13, rue des Gravilliers (3rd); Tel. 09 67 87 23 10 Tue-Sat 9.30am–5pm (6pm Fri-Sat)

Musée de la Chasse et de la Nature
→ 62, rue des Archives (3rd); Tel. 01 53 01 92 40 Tue-Sun 11am–6pm (9.30pm Wed)

Musée Cognacq-Jay
→ 8, rue Elzévir (3rd) Tel. 01 40 27 07 21 Tue-Sun 10am–6pm

Maison de Victor Hugo
→ 6, pl. des Vosges (4th) Tel. 01 42 72 10 16 Tue-Sun 10am–6pm

🏠 Garrice
→ 26, rue Saint-Antoine (4th); Tel. 01 42 72 35 48 Mon-Sat 10.30am (11am Mon)–7.30pm, Sun 2.30–7pm

🍷 Open Café
→ 17, rue des Archives (4th); Tel. 01 42 72 26 18 Daily 11am–2am

LE MARAIS WALK

Place de la République · RÉPUBLIQUE · Av. de la République · TEMPLE · Bd Voltaire · FILLES DU CALVAIRE · ST-SÉBASTIEN FROISSART · CHEMIN VERT · BASTILLE · Place de la Bastille

Musée des Arts et Métiers · La Gaîté Lyrique · RÉAUMUR SÉBASTOPOL · ARTS ET MÉTIERS · Le Carreau du Temple · Square du Temple · CAFÉ INEKO · Maison de N. Flamel · RAMBUTEAU · Marché des Enfants-Rouges · Musée d'Art et d'Histoire du judaïsme · Musée de la Chasse · Hôtel de Soubise · Musée Picasso · OPEN CAFÉ · HÔTEL DE VILLE · Musée Cognacq-Jay · Place de l'Hôtel-de-Ville · Saint-Gervais-Saint-Protais · L'ÉBOUILLANTÉ · MEP · SAINT-PAUL · Place des Vosges · Hôtel de Sully · Quartier Saint-Paul · Hôtel de Sens · GARRICE · ÎLE DE LA CITÉ · PONT MARIE · ÎLE SAINT-LOUIS · SEINE

0 — 200 m

CHÂTEAU DE VERSAILLES

Day trips within an hour of the city

BOIS DE VINCENNES
→ *Subway: Château-de-Vincennes*
Zoo: Tel. 0811 224 122; For opening times, see parczoologiquedeparis.fr
Fifteen minutes from the heart of Paris, with leafy lanes, a boating lake, a pagoda, a racetrack, a 14th-c. royal castle that is one of the tallest in Europe (165 ft) and the Parc Floral botanical gardens, spread over 76 acres. The zoo was refurbished in 2014, but it has preserved the artificial rock that plays host to its monkeys.

Les Officiers
→ *3, av. de Nogent, Vincennes*
Tel. 01 43 28 25 10; Daily 8am–midnight
Close to the Parc Floral and the castle. Salads, grilled meat and snacks; also has a terrace. Dishes €14–21; set lunch menu €15–19 (Mon-Fri); Sunday brunch €25.

BOIS DE BOULOGNE
→ *Subway: Porte-Maillot, Les Sablons, Porte-Dauphine; The Louis-Vuitton Foundation: 8, av. du Mahatma-Gandhi (16th); Tel. 01 40 69 96 00 Mon, Wed-Fri noon–7pm (9pm Fri); Sat-Sun 11am–8pm*

The city's second green lung, to the east, was laid out by Napoleon II with ponds, lanes and a waterfall. The Louis-Vuitton Foundation cultural center (**E** A3), resembling a series of glass sails puffed with air, was designed by Frank Gehry as a stage for contemporary art exhibitions. The Bois de Boulogne also contains the Parc de Bagatelle, with vast lawns and flower gardens arranged by species, including their famous roses. *See also page 11.*

Le Frank
→ *Tel. 01 58 44 25 70*
Wed-Mon noon–7pm (10pm Fri-Sat)
Opening times vary depending on exhibitions
The restaurant of the Fondation Louis-Vuitton. Dishes €22–38; set lunch menu €28. Also, inside the Bois de Boulogne is Le Chalet des îles (**F** A1).

SAINT-OUEN FLEA MARKET
→ *Subway: Porte de Clignancourt*
Sat-Sun 9am (10am Sun)–6pm; Mon 11am–7pm
Info point: 124, rue des Rosiers, Saint-Ouen
Tel. 01 55 87 67 50
This enormous, labyrinthine flea market on the northern outskirts of Paris is reputedly the largest of its kind in the world. It is in fact 14 separate markets in one: antiques,

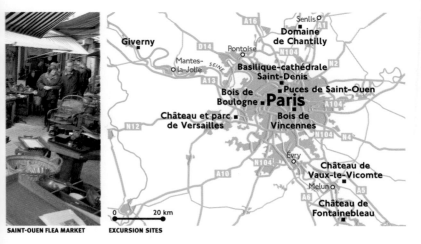

SAINT-OUEN FLEA MARKET   **EXCURSION SITES**

0   20 km

---

vintage furniture and clothing, jewelry, books,
industrial design, etc.

BASILIQUE-CATHÉDRALE SAINT-DENIS
→ *6 miles to the north; 1, rue de la Légion-d'Honneur
Subway: Basilique Saint-Denis; Tel. 01 48 09 83 54
Daily 10am (noon Sun)–6.15pm (5.15pm in winter)*
This Gothic masterpiece houses the tombs of
the kings of France and has superb funerary
art dating from the 12th to the 16th centuries.
La Bigoudène Café
→ *11, allée des Six Chapelles, Saint-Denis
Tel. 01 48 09 34 84; Mon-Sat 9am–5pm*
Three convivial spaces in one: a crêperie, tea
room and a deli. *Galettes* (Breton crêpes) €3–9.

CHÂTEAU AND PARC DE VERSAILLES
→ *13 miles to the west
RER C train to Versailles-Rive-Gauche; by train from
Gare Saint-Lazare to Versailles-Rive-Droite; Tel. 01 30
83 78 00; Tue-Sun 9am–6.30pm (5.30pm in winter)
Park: Daily 7am–8.30pm (8am–6pm in winter)*
The Sun King's extraordinary palace: inside, the
royal apartments and the dazzling Hall of Mirrors;
outside, the Petit and Grand Trianon (pavilions),
the Queen's Hamlet and, of course, the
spectacular gardens and groves.
La Petite Venise
→ *Allée d'Apollon (in the park of the château)*

*Tel. 01 39 53 25 69; April-Oct: Daily 11.45am–6pm
Nov-March: Tue-Sun 11.45am–5.30pm*
An elegant Italian restaurant with a take-out
service for picnics. Has a terrace surrounded
by rose trees. Dishes €16–23.

DOMAINE DE CHANTILLY
→ *25 miles to the north; RER D train from Gare du Nord
to Chantilly-Gouvieux, then 20 mins by foot (or taxi)
Tel. 03 44 27 31 80; April-Oct: Daily 10am–6pm (8pm
for park); Nov-March: Wed-Sun 11.30am–7pm*
The Chantilly Château (16th and 19th c.) is
the dramatic showcase for the Duc d'Aumale's
collection of paintings (Raphael, Poussin,
Watteau). Lavishly decorated apartments, the
largest stables in Europe (riding demonstrations/
shows) and 17th-century flowerbeds designed
by the royal gardener, André Le Nôtre.
Le Hameau
→ *Parc de Chantilly
Tel. 03 44 57 46 21; March-mid Nov: Daily noon–6pm
(closed Tue in March and Nov)*
A half-timbered cottage nestling amidst greenery.
Local specialties. Set menu €22–45.

CHÂTEAU DE VAUX-LE-VICOMTE
→ *35 miles to the southeast; train from Gare
de l'Est to Verneuil-L'Étang, then the 'châteaubus'
shuttle; Tel. 01 64 14 41 90; End March-beg Nov: Daily*

CHÂTEAU DE VAUX-LE-VICOMTE

10am–6pm; End Nov-beg Jan: Wed-Sun 11am–8pm (daily during Christmas holidays)
The sublime château commissioned by Nicolas Fouquet, one of Louis XIV's courtiers. Hosts magical candlelit evenings (May-Oct).

Le Relais de l'écureuil
→ In the château grounds; Tel. 01 64 14 41 90
End March-beg Nov: Daily 11am–5pm (11pm Sat May-beg Oct); end Nov-beg Jan: Wed-Sun 11am–5pm (daily during Christmas holidays)
A self-service area offers snacks but full meals are available on candlelit evenings. Set menu €20–25. More up-market is Les Charmilles, on the Terrasse des Communs (Sat nights May-early Oct; €57–76).

CHÂTEAU DE FONTAINEBLEAU
→ 44 miles to the southeast; train from Gare de Lyon to Fontainebleau-Avon, then bus no. 1
Tel. 01 60 71 50 70
Wed-Mon 9.30am–6pm (5pm Oct-March)
Originally a woodland manor used by Louis VII (1120–1180), Fontainebleau later became the favorite home of François I, who turned it into a Renaissance château and a showcase for art of the period (the Fontainebleau School would enjoy prestige throughout Europe). French kings would continue to spend time here, all the while redecorating

and restructuring the building – hence its somewhat piecemeal appearance. It still has a superb collection of furniture and painting, and the park is equally impressive.

La Petite Ardoise
→ 16, rue Montebello, Fontainebleau
Tel. 01 64 24 08 66; Tue-Sat noon–2pm, 7–10pm
A fine restaurant close to the château. Some dishes can be ordered as tapas-size portions. Dishes €19; set menu €19 (lunch), €33 (dinner).

GIVERNY
→ 44 miles to the northwest; train from Gare de Saint-Lazare to Vernon, then Fondation Claude-Monet shuttle; 84, rue Claude-Monet
Tel. 02 32 51 28 21
End March-beg Nov: Daily 9.30am–6pm
The 'painters' village', on the border with Normandy, contains the house where Monet lived for 43 years with its large studio, lush garden, water lilies and Japanese bridge.

Brasserie des artistes
→ 99, rue Claude-Monet
Tel. 02 32 51 94 61
End March-beg Nov: Daily 10am–6pm
A bright restaurant-tearoom inside the Museum of Impressionism (Giverny's other major cultural institution). Set menu €20.

PRACTICALITIES

All the essentials for your stay in Paris!

CITY PROFILE

- 2.2 million inhabitants in the city center
- 20 arrondissements
- 40 square miles
- The most visited city in the world: 29 million visitors each year
- 208 theaters, 144 museums, 10,000 cafés and restaurants, 1,600 hotels
- The River Seine: 8 miles and 37 bridges; its banks are a UNESCO World Heritage Site

VIEW FROM THE TOWERS OF NOTRE-DAME-DE-PARIS

Paris has a temperate climate and does not often experience excessive heat or cold, so it can be enjoyed all year round. June and September, which are the driest and sunniest, are the most appealing. Tourism is at its most intense in the summer, at Christmas and on weekends in May and June. Many Parisians leave town in August, and many small businesses are closed as a result.

WWW.

Paris online
➔ *parisinfo.com*
Website of the tourist office.
➔ *paris.fr*
The city's official website.
➔ *quefaire.paris.fr*
➔ *parisbouge.com*
➔ *sortiraparis.com*
Things to do and places to visit in the capital.
Internet cafés

Milk
➔ *31, bd Sébastopol (1st)*
(**B** C2)
➔ *5, rue d'Odessa (14th)*
(**G** B3)
Open 24/7.

TOURIST INFORMATION

Paris Tourist Offices (**B** C3)
➔ *29, rue de Rivoli (4th)*
Daily 9am (10am in winter)–7pm
Information, reservations, excursions and ticket sales. Also at Gare du Nord (**D** D4) and Carrousel du Louvre, *99, rue de Rivoli* (**C** A3). The Montmartre Union of Initiative (independent) is at *7, rue Drevet montmartre-guide.com*

TELEPHONE

Useful numbers
Police

Tel. 17
Pompiers (fire brigade)
➔ *Tel. 18*
Samu (ambulance)
➔ *Tel. 15 or 112 (cell phone)*
Directory inquiries
➔ *Tel. 118 712 / 118 218*
Lost property
➔ *Tel. 08 21 00 25 25*

DIARY OF EVENTS

March–May
Banlieues Bleues
➔ *Mid March–mid April;*
banlieuesbleues.org
Jazz festival in Seine-St-Denis (northern suburbs).
Paris Marathon
➔ *April; parismarathon.com*
Museum Night
➔ *Mid May*
nuitdesmusees.culture.gouv.fr
Tours by night; free entry.
June
Paris Jazz Festival
➔ *Weekends during June–July*
parisjazzfestival.fr

In the Parc de Vincennes.
Fête de la Musique
➔ *June 21*
fetedelamusique.culture.fr
Free concerts all over the city; listings in the daily newspapers.
Gay Pride
➔ *End June; gaypride.fr*
Famous parade, from Montparnasse to Bastille.
Festival Solidays
➔ *Three days, last weekend in June; solidays.org*
➔ *Associations and artists for AIDS awareness gather at Longchamp racecourse.*
July–August
National Day
➔ *July 13 (evening) and 14*
Firemen's ball: military parade down the Champs-Élysées and fireworks.
Paris Quartiers d'Été
➔ *Mid July–beg Aug*
quartierdete.com
Theater, dance, concerts in all the city's districts.
La Villette Film Festival
➔ *Mid July–mid Aug*

LUTETIA TO PARIS

52 BC Roman legions conquer the Parisii **508** Clovis makes Paris the capital city of the Franks **1572** St Bartholomew's Day Massacre **1789** Fall of the Bastille **1841** Thiers builds a defensive wall around Paris, defining the city limits **1860** Haussmann rebuilds much of the city, which moves from 12 to 20 arrondissements **May 1871** The Commune: Paris in revolt **1900** Olympic Games and Universal Exhibition **Aug 1944** Liberation of Paris **May 1968** Barricades in the Latin Quarter

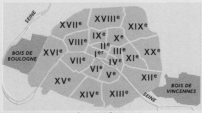

THE ARRONDISSEMENTS (DISTRICTS) OF PARIS

A CAFÉ ON RUE MOUFFETARD

In the Parc de la Villette (**J** C2), the largest open-air movie theater in Paris.
Paris-Plages
→ *Four to five weeks, mid July-end Aug*
Sand, umbrellas and deckchairs are imported to the banks of the Seine and the Parc de la Villette lake to create beaches.
September
Jazz à la Villette
→ *First two weeks*
jazzalavillette.com
Eclectic jazz and performance art in the Parc de la Villette.
Fête des Jardins
→ *One weekend end Sep*
Garden show with guided tours, walks, workshops.
Heritage Open Days
→ *Third weekend*
journeesdupatrimoine.culture.gouv.fr
Free entry to monuments usually closed to the public.
Festival d'Automne

→ *Mid Sep-end Dec*
festival-automne.com
Dance, theater, music.
October
Fête des Vendanges de Montmartre
→ *Usually on a weekend*
In the private vineyard of a monastery, the neighborhood comes together in a parade to celebrate the distinctive vintage that its grapes produce.
Nuit Blanche
→ *Early Oct (7pm–7am)*
A night of free cultural events in some unusual places (swimming pools, churches, libraries, etc.).
Foire Internationale d'Art Contemporain (FIAC)
→ *5 days end Oct; fiac.com*
France's most important contemporary art event.

BUDGET

A double room in a two-star hotel: €70–120;

main course in a brasserie: €12–20; set menu in a neo-bistro: €30–35; museum entry: €7–13; a beer: €2.50–4.50; an espresso: €1.50–3; entry to a club: €10–25.

OPENING TIMES

Shops
→ *Mon-Sat 10am–7pm (sometimes closed on Mon, except department stores; late opening on Thu in large department stores)*
Museums
→ *Usually 10am–6pm City museums usually close on Mon, national museums on Tue*
Parks and gardens
→ *Usually daily 8am (9am Sat-Sun)–sunset*
Banks
→ *Mon-Sat 9am–4/5pm*
Open 24/7
Pharmacie Européenne (**D** A4)
→ *6, place de Clichy (9th)*

ARCHITECTURE

Gothic Paris
(12th–early 16th c.)
High Gothic chapels, ogival vaulted ceilings and Gothic arches; Notre-Dame (**A** E2).
Classical Paris
(17th–18th c.)
Townhouses and other impressive buildings: symmetry and sobriety of decor; Invalides (**F** F2).
Haussmann's Paris
(second half of 19th c.)
Préfet from 1853 to 1870, Baron Haussmann modified the city's urban landscape, which had remained unchanged since the Middle Ages. He introduced the use of freestone, improvements to the sewage system, created parks and gardens, and the Grands Boulevards (large thoroughfares); Boulevard St-Germain (**A** A2-E3), Luxembourg Gardens (**A** B3).
Art Nouveau Paris
(1893–1912)
Mix of innovative materials, curved forms and asymmetry, dear to Hector Guimard; Abbesses subway station (**D** B4).
Art Deco Paris
(1912–39)
Pure, geometric shapes and solid composition of volumes; Palais de Chaillot (**F** D1).
Contemporary Paris
Post-modernist; Bibliothèque Nationale de France (**H** C4); Musée du Quai-Branly – Jacques-Chirac (**F** D1); Fondation Louis-Vuitton (off map **E** A3).

JARDIN DES TUILERIES

STEPS IN MONTMARTRE

Tel. 01 48 74 65 18
Pharmacy.
Poste du Louvre (B A2)
➔ 52, rue du Louvre (1st)
Tel. 36 31; Daily 7.30am–6pm
Central post office.
Restaurant Au Pied de Cochon (B A2)
➔ 6, rue Coquillière (1st)
Tel. 01 40 13 77 00

EATING OUT

Establishments
Boulangerie (bakery)
For croissants, *pains au chocolat*, baguettes and sandwiches.
Bistro
For a quick snack (*croque-monsieur*), salads, cheese and charcuterie).
Neo-bistro
The French version of the British gastropub; good-quality, modern takes on traditional dishes.
Brasserie
Steak and fries, *choucroute* and other typical dishes.

Restaurant
French or foreign cuisine and often a well-stocked cellar. Reserve.
Food trucks
These are becoming increasingly popular, serving anything from burgers (Cantine California, Le Camion Qui Fume) to focaccia (Mozza & Co), crêpes, pizzas and fish & chips, as well as street food from Venezuela, Mexico, Vietnam... The trucks' locations are announced on their websites and social media sites. .
Cookery classes
Cook-and-taste workshops for many types of cuisine.
Atelier des Chefs
Offers a wide choice; four locations in Paris.
➔ atelierdeschefs.fr
École Lenôtre
Cook school of the famous caterer.
➔ lenotre.com

*Yachts de Paris, quai Henri-IV (**I** A3); 22, av. de la Porte de Vincennes (off map **I** F3).*

SIGHTSEEING

For ways to see the city for free or at a reduced cost, and for details of sightseeing passes, see *Paris on a Budget*, p. 16.
Children
Some museums offer games, tours, workshops.
Concessions
Usually for students, 18–25-year-olds, the over 60s and the unemployed.
Museums
Benefit from fewer crowds by visiting a museum in the evening: most have a later closing time one day a week.

GREEN SPACES

Paris has over 460 parks and gardens. See the

Day Trips pages.
Bois de Boulogne (F A1-3)
Bicycle rental at the Jardin d'Acclimatation entrance.
Bois de Vincennes (off I F4)
Cycle tracks, bridlepaths and pedestrian pathways.

SHOWS

Reservations
Fnac
➔ Tel. 08 92 68 36 22
fnacspectacles.com
For tickets to the theater, concerts, festivals, etc.
Programs
Officiel des Spectacles, Télérama Sortir
Listings of cultural events; out every Wed, on sale at newsagents.

OUT AND ABOUT

Latin Quarter and **St-Germain (A** C2):
Jazzy, student quarter

JARDIN TINO-ROSSI

with interesting streets and the atmosphere that goes with a lively university district.
Le Marais (B D3)
Winding medieval lanes; eclectic community; lively bars.
Pigalle (D B4)
The epicenter of Parisian nightlife; one of the city's fashionable final frontiers.
Oberkampf (I B1)
Row upon row of humming shabby-chic bars along Rue Oberkampf and surrounding streets.
Canal Saint-Martin (J A4)
A waterway and a fashionable area of the city. Busy, with a bobo crowd and lots of popular hangouts. In the spring and summer, locals come in droves to the banks of the canal to picnic and strum guitars waterside.
Ménilmontant (J C5)
Thriving centre of alternative Paris; lively

arts and music venues.
Bastille (I B2)
History-rich neighborhood; classic Parisian nightlife.
Bibliothèque (H D4)
for barge-concerts, with deckchairs on the quaysides in summer.

SHOPPING

Sales
In January and end of June-July.
Department stores
Le BHV Marais (B C3)
→ 52, rue de Rivoli (4th)
Mon-Sat 9.30am–8pm;
Sun 11am–7.30pm
A diverse range.
Galeries Lafayette (D A6)
→ 35-40 bd Haussmann (9th); Mon-Sat 9.30am–8.30pm; Sun 11am–8pm
Printemps (D A6)
→ 64, bd Haussmann (9th)
Mon-Sat 9.30am–8pm (8.45pm Thu); Sun 11am–7pm

Galeries Lafayette and Printemps are the largest and most luxurious department stores.
Le Bon Marché (G B1)
→ 24, rue de Sèvres (7th)
Mon-Sat 10am–8pm (8.45pm Thu); Sun 11am–7.45pm
The most elegant.
Flea markets
St-Ouen
(off **D** A1)
→ Subway: Porte-de-Clignancourt
Sat-Sun 9am (10am Sun)–6pm; Mon 11am–5pm
The oldest and largest of the city's flea markets.
See also Day Trips (**L**).
Montreuil (off **I** F2)
→ Subway: Porte-de-Montreuil; Sat-Mon 7am–7.30pm
With St-Ouen, the most popular market (cheap clothes and knick-knacks).
Vanves (off **G** A5)
→ Av. M. Sangnier and G.Lafenestre

Subway: Porte-de-Vanves
Sat-Sun 7am–7.30pm
Interesting bric-à-brac and reasonably priced antiques.
Food markets
For a complete list, see paris.fr/marches
Place Maubert (A D3)
→ Tue, Thu, Sat 7am–2.30pm (3pm Sun)
Bd R.-Lenoir (I B2)
→ Thu, Sun 7am–2.30pm (3pm Sun)
Rue d'Aligre (I C3)
→ Tue-Sun 7.30am–1.30pm (2.30pm Sat-Sun)
Bd de Belleville (J B5)
→ Tue, Fri 7am–2.30pm
Bd de la Chapelle (D D4)
→ Wed 8am–1pm; Sat 7am–3pm
Flower markets
Pl. de la Madeleine (C C1)
→ Mon-Sat 8am–7.30pm (depending on the season)
Pl. Louis-Lépine, Île de la Cité (A D2)
→ Daily 8am–7.30pm (7pm Sun)

22

AIRPORTS

➜ *Tel. 39 50*
aeroportsdeparis.fr
All practical information
for both Roissy and Orly
airports.

**Roissy-Charles-
de-Gaulle (CDG)**
Three terminals: 1, 2
(regular flights) and 3
(charter flights).

Orly (ORY)
Four terminals: 1, 2, 3
and 4.

**Paris-Beauvais-Tillé
(BVA)**
➜ *Tel. 08 92 68 20 66*
Shuttles to Porte Maillot
(E B2); €16; 75–90 mins
aeroportbeauvais.com
Used by low-cost
airlines.

ACCESS TO AIRPORTS

AIRPORT – CENTER

From Roissy-CDG
RER B (train): *€10.30*
Roissybus: *Rue Scribe, by
Opéra subway* **(C** D1); €12
Le Bus Direct:
Porte Maillot **(E** B2), *Étoile*
(E C3), *Trocadéro* **(F** D1),
Eiffel Tower **(F** D1),
Montparnasse **(G** B3),
Gare de Lyon **(H** C2); €18
Taxi: *approx. €50*
From Orly
Orlyval: *Orlyval then
RER B; €12.10*
Orlybus: *In front of RER
Denfert-Rochereau* **(G** C4)
€8.30
Le Bus Direct: *Étoile,
Trocadéro, Montparnasse*
€12
Taxi: *approx. €35*

ACCOMMODATION

*Unless otherwise stated,
the prices given are for a
standard double room en
suite, without breakfast. It is
recommended to reserve at
least a month in advance. For
information, see the tourist
office website: parisinfo.com*

CAMPING

**Camping Indigo
Paris (F** A1)
➜ *2, allée du Bord-de-l'Eau
(16th); Tel. 01 45 24 30 00
campingparis.fr*
Situated on a natural
7-hectare park in the
Bois de Boulogne, this
campsite on the banks of
the Seine has a bright and
modern central lodge, a
café-restaurant and free
internet points. 415
pitches (€27.60–39.60),
over 75 cottages and
gyspy-style caravans
(from €97 for 4 people).

YOUTH HOSTELS

**St-Christopher's
Inn (J** B2)
➜ *159, rue de Crimée (19th)
Tel. 01 40 34 34 40
st-christophers.co.uk*
A hostel situated in one of
the former warehouses
known as the Magasins
Généraux. Four- to 12-bed
dormitories and double
rooms (some en suite).
Restaurant, bar, internet
café. Also at *7, rue de
Dunkerque,* between Gare
du Nord and Gare de l'Est.
Double room €40–120;
dorm €21.80–40/pers.

Hostel Oops ! (H A4)
➜ *50, av. des Gobelins
(13th); Tel. 01 47 07 47 00
oops-paris.com*
A bright hostel with
double rooms and large
dorms. Double room €70–
115; dorm €27–43/pers.

Generator (J B4)
➜ *9, pl. du Colonel-Fabien
(10th); Tel. 01 70 98 84 00*
generatorhostels.com
A large, hip youth
hostel. Inventive decor
and services (bar, roof
terrace, laundromat,
travel shop). Double
room €80–180; dorm
from €17/pers.

Hôtels MIJE (B D4)
➜ *6, rue de Fourcy;
11, rue du Fauconnier; 12,
rue des Barres (4th);
Tel.01 42 74 23 45; mije.com*
In the heart of the
Marais, three hostels in
characterful buildings.
Stays limted to 7 nights.
Single room €55; double
room €82; dorm (4–10
people) €33.50/pers
breakfast included.

Les Piaules (J B5)
➜ *59, bd de Belleville (11th)
Tel. 01 43 55 09 97
espiaules.com*
Modern youth hostel,
extending from a bar-
café at street level to a
roof terrace. Thirty-four
rooms and dormitories

(2–8 people). Double
room €100–140; dorm
from €20–40/pers.

UNDER €100

Hôtel Tolbiac (H B5)
➜ *122, rue de Tolbiac (13th)
Tel. 01 44 24 25 54
hotel-tolbiac.com*
Bright and modern hotel
with 47 rooms. €59–79.

Hôtel des Arts (I C2)
➜ *2 rue Godefroy-
Cavaignac (11th)
Tel. 01 43 79 72 57
paris-hotel-desarts.com*
In the heart of this lively
area, a building decorated
in street-art style has 35
light and airy rooms, some
of which are decorated
with murals. €65–250.

Hôtel Eldorado (E F1)
➜ *18, rue des Dames (17th)
Tel. 01 45 22 35 21
eldoradohotel.fr*
Attractive hotel laid out
around a leafy courtyard.
The decor derives from

TRAINS/STATIONS

SNCF information
National network
→ Tel. 36 35; oui.sncf
Suburban network
→ transilien.com
Trains serving the areas around Paris, notably Giverny, Fontainebleau, etc.

Train stations
Six stations for suburban and national networks: Gare du Nord (north), Gare de l'Est (northeast), Gare de Lyon (southeast), Gare d'Austerlitz (southwest, southeast), Gare Montparnasse (west, southwest), Gare Saint-Lazare (northeast).

THE ELEVATED RAILWAY, LINE 6

TRAM, AT THE PORTE DE VERSAILLES

TAXIS

Taxis display a green light when free, a red one when occupied.
Taxis G7
→ Tel. 36 07
Alpha Taxis
→ Tel. 01 45 85 85 85

SELF-SERVICE BIKES

Velib'
→ Tel. 01 76 49 12 34
velib-metropole.fr
Numerous stations for rented bicycles (some electric), around 320 yards apart, in Paris and the neighboring communes. Charges depend on the service chosen and frequency of use. €1/30 min no subscription, or €3.10/month or €37.20/year, with the first half-hour free (€8.30/month and €99.60/year for mechanical and electric bikes)

Other services
Velib' now has many competitors with shared, 'free-floating' bike services with no subscription, each distinguished by its own particular colors. Their apps can be downloaded to a cellphone.

SCOOTERS

Cityscoot
→ cityscoot.eu
Self-service electric scooters (with helmet included), with no stations. Download the app to locate and use the scooters (7am–midnight); €0.29/min.

---

items picked up by the owners on their travels. Excellent Bistro des Dames downstairs at street level. €80–150.

Hôtel de Nesle (A C2)
→ 7, rue de Nesle (6th)
Tel. 01 43 54 62 41
hoteldenesleparis.com
A quirky hotel in a prime location where the owner has decorated each of the 18 rooms with murals to illustrate such themes as Molière, Africa and the Orient. Rooms overlook either the peaceful street outside or a wonderful rustic garden to the rear. €85–130.

Hôtel du Nord (J A5)
→ 47, rue Albert-Thomas (10th)
Tel. 01 42 01 66 00
hoteldunord-leparivelo.com
A hotel full of charm near the Canal St-Martin, with 23 clean, cheerful rooms. Bicycles available for guests' use. €86.

Solar Hôtel (G B4)
→ 22, rue Boulard (14th)
Tel. 01 43 21 08 20
solarhotel.fr
This eco-hotel has set a benchmark in green hotel accommodation in Paris: solar panels, recycling and no WiFi in the 34 rooms. There's a small, leafy courtyard and bicycles for guests' use. €89 (organic breakfast included).

Mama Shelter (I E2)
→ 109, rue de Bagnolet (20th); Tel. 01 43 48 48 48
mamashelter.com
A state-of-the-art hotel in the district of St-Blaise. It has 172 rooms with all comforts. From €89.

€100–150

La Maison Montparnasse (G A4)
→ 53, rue de Gergovie (14th)
Tel. 01 45 42 11 39
lamaisonmontparnasse.com
In a small street in the Pernety district, a modern hotel of great charm with 36 rooms (8 are triples). €105–135.

Hôtel Saint-André-des-Arts (A C2)
→ 66, rue Saint-André-des-Arts (6th)
Tel. 01 43 26 96 16
hotel-saintandredesarts.fr
In an ancient mansion house, 31 characterful rooms with exposed wooden beams; those giving onto the street are the brightest. Homemade breakfast. €105–138.

Ermitage Sacré-Cœur (D C3)
→ 24, rue Lamarck (18th)
Tel. 01 42 64 79 22
ermitagesacrecoeur.fr
An elegant 19th-century townhouse with five stylish bedrooms and three comfortable apartments. Beautiful printed fabrics on the

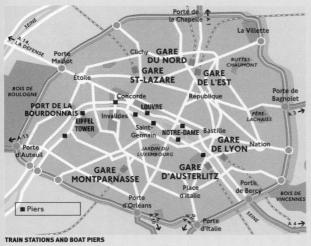

TRAIN STATIONS AND BOAT PIERS

■ Piers

PARIS BY BOAT

Bateaux-mouches
Batobus
→ *Tel. 08 25 05 01 01*
€16/€18 (one-/two-day pass)
The Eiffel Tower to the Jardin des Plantes.
Bateaux parisiens
→ *At the foot of the Eiffel Tower; €14*
To the île de la Cité.
Canauxrama
→ *Tel. 01 42 39 15 00;*
€12–18
Cruises on the canals.
Compagnie des Bateaux-Mouches
→ *Tel. 01 42 25 96 10*
bateaux-mouches.fr
For lunch or dinner on the Seine.

walls, carved wooden beds and a lovely garden. €110 (apartment €130–170).

Hôtel Esmeralda (A D2)
→ *4, rue Saint-Julien-le-Pauvre (5th)*
Tel. 01 43 54 19 20
hotel-esmeralda.fr
This 17th-century townhouse leads onto the pretty Vivienne square and houses a charming 19-room hotel with exposed stone walls and velvet sofas. Rooms on the street side have views of Notre-Dame. €125–145.

Familia Hôtel (A D3)
→ *11, rue des Écoles (5th)*
Tel. 01 43 54 55 27
familiahotel.com
A well-kept, family-run hotel since 1930, with exposed beams and stonework. Next door, at no. 13, the more expensive Hôtel Minerve, owned by the same

people) has larger rooms. €134–190.

Hôtel des Grandes Écoles (A D4)
→ *75, rue du Cardinal-Lemoine (5th)*
Tel. 01 43 26 79 23
hotel-grandes-ecoles.com
A rare thing in the middle of Paris: a villa resembling a country manor with a private garden. The décor of this 19th-century bourgeois house is immaculate, with antique furniture and floral wallpaper. €140–170.

OVER 150€

Hôtel Paradis (D D6)
→ *41, rue des Petites-Écuries (10th);*
Tel. 01 45 23 08 22
hotelparadisparis.com
A smart boutique hotel with the stamp of the designer of the moment, Dorothée Meilichzon,

mixing minimalist and retro styles in its 38 rooms (some of which overlook Montmartre). €150–220.

Color Design Hôtel (I C3)
→ *35, rue de Cîteaux (12th)*
Tel. 01 43 07 77 28
colordesign-hotel-paris.com
As its name implies, the focus is on light, color and design in this hotel's 46 stylish, modern rooms with all conveniences. €150–235.

Hôtel Amour (D B5)
→ *8, rue de Navarin (9th)*
Tel. 01 48 78 31 80
hotelamourparis.fr
An unusual hotel, with 24 rooms designed by artists or by the owners themselves. It has a terraced winter garden and a popular café-restaurant. Along the same lines is the Grand Amour hotel, with 42 rooms, on *18, rue de la Fidélité* **(D** D5). €150–390.

Hôtel des Grands Hommes (A D4)
→ *17, pl. du Panthéon (5th)*
Tel. 01 46 34 19 60
hotelsdesgrandshommes.com
An elegant 18th-century hotel in a prime location, with 30 rooms. Views of the Pantheon dome from the balconies of the deluxe rooms. €160–340.

Hôtel du Petit Moulin (B E2)
→ *29-31, rue du Poitou (3rd)*
Tel. 01 42 74 10 10
hotelpetitmoulinparis.com
Beyond its picturesque fin-de-siècle façade, the reception area was formerly the oldest bakery in Paris, dating back to the 16th century. In contrast to this, the 17 bedrooms were designed by Christian Lacroix to create an ambience that is at once stylish, imaginative and very comfortable. €185–495.

BUS STOP, NOTRE-DAME

AEDICULE BY HECTOR GUIMARD, AT PORTE DAUPHINE STATION

PUBLIC TRANSPORT

RATP information
→ ratp.fr

Bus
→ *Daily 6.30am–8.30pm (12.30am for some lines)*
59 lines; reduced service Sun and public holidays.

Noctilien
→ *Daily 12.30am–5.30am*
Night bus; 47 lines.

Tramway
→ *Daily 5.30am–12.30am (2am Fri-Sat)*
Two lines in Paris: T3a, between the Garigliano Bridge and Porte de Vincennes; and T3b, from Porte de Vincennes to Porte d'Asnières.

Métro (subway)
→ *Daily 5.30am–12.30am (1.30/2am Fri-Sat)*
Nearly 300 stations and 16 lines (numbered 1 to 14, with two secondary lines) in Paris and the suburbs (zones 1 and 2).

RER
→ *Daily 5.30am–12.30am*
Five fast lines (A, B, C, D, E) across Paris and Île-de-France (zones 1-5).

Tickets and passes
Tickets
→ *€1.90 single (€2 onboard); €14.90 for ten*
From subway stations (ticket machines) and some newsagent stores.

Mobilis
→ *€7.50–17.80 (depending on the zones)*
Unlimited journeys; valid for one day only.

Paris Visite
→ *€12–65.80 (depending on no. of days and zones)*
Pass for all modes of transport, plus reduced prices to various sights. See also *Paris on a Budget* (p. 16)

25 Hours Hotel Terminus Nord (**D** D5)
→ *12, bd de Denain (10th)*
Tel. 01 42 80 20 00
25hours-hotels.com
In an atmospheric building dating back to the 1860s, this exuberant hotel reflects the cosmopolitanism of the neighborhood: boldly patterned textiles in the rooms, a restaurant with Arab and Asian flavors, and a bar decorated in contemporary African style. €195–280.

Hôtel des Marronniers (**A** B2)
→ *21, rue Jacob (6th)*
Tel. 01 43 25 30 60
hoteldesmarronniers.com
A hotel full of charm and character in a pretty street. Rooms open onto the courtyard, the bell tower of the church of St Germain or the garden. The latter, also a tearoom, is a haven of tranquility.

€230–270.

Hôtel de Londres-Eiffel (**F** E1)
→ *1, rue Augereau (7th)*
Tel. 01 45 51 63 02
londres-eiffel.com
The French idea of an English country cottage, with 30 small but beautifully decorated rooms, four of which overlook the Eiffel Tower. €245–360.

LUXURY HOTELS

Smart dress is required if you go to one of the following hotels for drinks or brunch

Hôtel de Crillon (**C** C2)
→ *10, pl. de la Concorde (8th)*
Tel. 01 44 71 15 00
crillon.com
A beautiful 18th-century palace, with marble on all floors and Baccarat crystal chandeliers. There is a private terrace that

offers views out to the Eiffel Tower and the Grand Palais. From €970.

Ritz (**C** D2)
→ *15, pl. Vendôme (1st)*
Tel. 01 43 16 30 30
ritzparis.com
The sumptuous and legendary townhouse (1898) on Place Vendôme, where Coco Chanel took a suite in 1937 and ended up staying for 34 years. Her suite has been preserved intact and is available for hire. From €1,000.

Le Meurice (**C** D2)
→ *228 rue de Rivoli (1st)*
Tel. 01 44 58 10 10
lemeurice.com
The first palace hotel in Paris, located minutes from the Louvre. This regal hotel is grand yet not stuffy – the artists Dalí and Warhol used to stay here. Two-star Michelin restaurant. From €800.

USEFUL WORDS AND PHRASES

Basics
Yes : oui
No : non
Hello/good morning/ good afternoon : bonjour
Hi/hello : salut
Good bye : au revoir
How are you? Comment allez-vous?
Please : S'il vous plaît
Merci : Thank you
You're welcome, it's a pleasure : Je vous en prie
Excuse me, sorry : Excusez-moi
Je ne parle pas français : I don't speak French
I don't understand : Je ne comprends pas
How much does it cost? Combien ça coûte?
Is there... ? Y a-t-il...?
Where is... ? Où est...?
What time is it? Quelle heure est-il?
I would like... Je voudrais...

Time and numbers
Today : aujourd'hui
Yesterday : hier
Tomorrow : demain
Morning : matin
Afternoon : après-midi
Evening : soir
What time is it? Quelle heure est-il?
It is ten o'clock : Il est dix heures
At noon : à midi
At midnight : à minuit
Monday : lundi
Tuesday : mardi
Wednesday : mercredi
Thursday : jeudi
Friday : vendredi
Saturday : samedi
Sunday : dimanche
One : un
Two : deux
Three : trois

Four : quatre
Five : cinq
Six : six
Seven : sept
Eight : huit
Nine : neuf
Ten : dix
Eleven : onze
Twelve : douze
Thirteen : treize
Fourteen : quatorze
Fifteen : quinze
Sixteen : seize
Seventeen : dix-sept
Eighteen : dix-huit
Nineteen : dix-neuf
Twenty : vingt
One hundred : cent
One thousand : mille

Transport
Airport : aéroport
Aeroplane : avion
Flight : vol
Subway : métro
Bus : bus
Bus stop : arrêt de bus
Boat : bateau
Taxi : taxi
Taxi rank : station de taxis
Coach : car
Train : train
Train station : gare
Coach station : gare routière
Bicycle, bike : vélo
Car : voiture
Adult : adulte
Child(ren) : enfant(s)
One-way ticket : aller
Return ticket : aller-retour
Driver's license : permis de conduire

Landmarks
Street, road : rue
Square : place
House : maison
Bridge : pont
Tower : tour
Town, city : ville
Castle : château
Market : marché

Museum : musée
Church : église
City hall : mairie
Tourist office : office de tourisme

Directions/orientation
To the left : à gauche
To the right : à droite
Straight ahead : tout droit
Route, trip : trajet
Map, plan : carte
Near : proche
Far : loin
Between : entre
Opposite : en face
In front of : devant
Behind : derrière
Next to : à côté de
I am looking for.... : Je cherche....
I am lost : Je me suis perdu(e)

Signage
Open : ouvert
Closed : fermé
Entrance, way in : entrée
Exit, way out : sortie
Lift : ascenseur
Stairs : escalier
Push : pousser
Pull : tirer
Ground floor : rdc
First/second floor : premier/deuxième étage
Restroom : toilettes
Men : hommes
Women : femmes
No entry : interdit

Eating out
Do you have a table for two? Avez-vous une table pour deux?
Could you give me the bill, please? Pouvez-vous me donner l'addition, s'il vous plaît?
Eat-in : sur place
Take-away : à emporter
Hot chocolate : chocolat chaud
Orange juice : jus

d'orange
Red / rosé / white wine : vin rouge / rosé / blanc
Beer : bière
Starter : entrée
Main course : plat principal
Dessert : dessert
Menu : carte
Dish of the day, special : plat du jour
Tap water : eau du robinet

Accommodation
Youth hostel : Auberge de jeunesse
Single / double room : chambre simple / double
Full : complet
Shower / bath : douche / baignoire
Sheet : drap
Pillow : oreiller
Blanket : couverture
Breakfast included : petit déjeuner inclus
Booking : réservation
I would like to reserve a room for two nights : Je voudrais reserver une chambre pour deux nuits

Communication
Phone : téléphone
Mobile phone : portable
Laptop : ordinateur portable
Password : mot de passe

Money matters
Money : argent
Free : gratuit
Concession : tarif réduit
Cash machine, ATM : distributeur
Credit card : carte bancaire / carte de crédit
Price : prix
Note : billet de banque
Change : monnaie
Coin : pièce de monnaie
Identification document : pièce d'identité

Entries are followed by a map reference, the first letter of which, in bold (**A, B, C...**), refers to the corresponding area and fold-out map. Entries followed by the symbol ✪ are featured in *Unmissable Sights* (pages 2–11).

M RER
Paris
RATP
ratp.fr

Propriété de la RATP - Agence Cartographique - PMI 01-2018 - JG - Design : bdcconseil - Reproduction interdite

Asnières–Gennevilliers **13**
Les Courtilles

Les Agnettes
Gabriel Péri
Saint-Ouen

Carrefo
Ple

Mairie
de St-Ouen

Garibaldi

J

Mairie
de Clichy
Porte
de Clichy

Porte
de St-Ouen
de Cl

Guy
Môquet

La
Caulai
Ab

Brochant

L

Pont de Levallois 3
Bécon

Anatole France
Louise Michel
Porte de Champerret
Pereire–Levallois

La Fourche

Blanche

Pereire

Wagram
Malesherbes

Rome
Place
de Clichy

A
L
U

1 La Défense
Grande Arche

Esplanade
de La Défense

Pont de Neuilly
Les Sablons

Porte Maillot
Neuilly–Porte Maillot

Argentine

2 Porte
Dauphine

Avenue Foch

Monceau

Courcelles

Ternes

Villiers

Liège

Europe

St-G

Trinité
d'Estienne
d'Orves

Notre-
de-Lo

6

Charles
de Gaulle
Étoile

Gare St-Lazare
St-Lazare 14

St-Augustin

Miromesnil
St-Philippe
du-Roule

E **Haussmann**
St-Lazare

Chaussée d'Anti
La Fayette

Victor Hugo

Kléber

George V
Franklin
D. Roosevelt

Havre
Caumartin

Opéra

Roissy

Quat

Boissière

Iéna

Alma
Marceau

Champs
Élysées
Clemenceau

Concorde

Madeleine

Pyramides

Palais Royal
Musée du
Louvre

Louvre
Rivoli

Avenue
Henri
Martin

Rue
de la Pompe

Trocadéro

Pont
de l'Alma

Invalides

Tuileries

Musée d'Orsay

Pont

La Muette

Passy

La Tour Maubourg

Assemblée Nationale

Boulainvilliers

Champ de Mars
Tour Eiffel
Bir-Hakeim

École
Militaire

Varenne

Solférino

Saint
François
Xavier

Rue
du Bac

St-Germain
des-Prés

Ranelagh

Avenue du
Pdt Kennedy

Dupleix

La Motte
Picquet
Grenelle

Sèvres
Babylone

Mabil
St-Sulp

Jasmin

Avenue
Émile Zola

Vaneau

Michel-Ange
Auteuil
Porte
d'Auteuil

Église
d'Auteuil

Javel

Charles
Michels

Cambronne

Commerce

Ségur

Duroc

Rennes

St-Placide
Montparnasse
Bienvenüe

No
des
Va

Mirabeau

Michel-Ange
Molitor

Chardon
Lagache
Exelmans

Javel
André
Citroën

Félix Faure

Sèvres
Lecourbe

Falguière

Pasteur

Edgar
Quinet

10

Marcel
Sembat

Porte
de St-Cloud

Pont
du Garigliano

Boucicaut

Gare
Montparnasse

Gaîté

Boulogne
Pont de St-Cloud

Boulogne
Jean Jaurès

Billancourt

Volontaires

Vaugirard

Pernety

9 Pont
de Sèvres

8 Balard

Issy
Val de Seine

Convention

Porte de Versailles

Plaisance

Pte de Vanves

Po
d'Orlé

Issy

Corentin Celton

N

12 Mairie d'Issy

Malakoff
Plateau de Vanves
Malakoff
Rue Étienne Dolet

Mair
de Montroug

An

C

Châtillon–Montrouge 13

B

Brochant (C)

30